S0-DIT-391

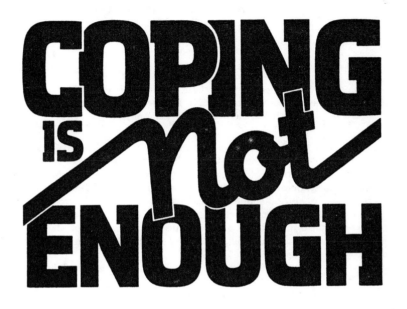

COPING IS not ENOUGH

Kendrick Strong

BROADMAN PRESS
Nashville, Tennessee

© Copyright 1987 • Broadman Press
All Rights Reserved
4250-42
ISBN: 0-8054-5042-4

Dewey Decimal Classification: 248.4
Subject Headings: CHRISTIAN LIFE
Library of Congress Catalog Number: 86-23260
Printed in the United States of America

Unless otherwise stated, all Scripture quotations are from the Revised Standard Version of the Bible, copyrighted 1946, 1952, © 1971, 1973.
Scripture quotations marked NEB are from *The New English Bible.* Copyright © The Delegates of the Oxford University Press and the Syndics of the Cambridge University Press, 1961, 1970. Reprinted by permission.
Scripture quotations marked KJV are from the King James Version of the Bible.
Scripture quotations marked Phillips are reprinted with permission of Macmillan Publishing Co., Inc. from J. B. Phillips: *The New Testament in Modern English,* Revised Edition. © J. B. Phillips 1958, 1960, 1972.
Scripture quotations marked VV are The *Vernacular Version,* © 1982 by John Kendrick Strong.

Library of Congress Cataloging-in-Publication Data
Strong, Kendrick.
 Coping is not enough.

  1. Christian life—1960— 2. Conduct of
life. I. Title.
BV4501.2.S7975 1987   248.4   86-23260
ISBN 0-8054-5042-4

BELMONT COLLEGE LIBRARY

122691

3V
501.2
S7975
987

To Ilo,
who more than
copes

Contents

Introduction

1. Cling Boldly to the Fact that God Loves You 11

2. Locate a Place Where God and You May Meet 17

3. Convert Your Whole Life into One Holy Ground 21

4. Continuously Orient Yourself Toward the Divine Light 25

5. Let God Become an Occupying Power 29

6. Rejoice in God's Providence 35

7. Rediscover the Historic Jesus 39

8. Rediscover the Contemporary Jesus 45

9. Utilize the Divine Chemistry of the Cross 51

10. Put on the Insignia of Jesus 55

11. Leave Elbowroom for the Holy Spirit 61

12. Believe in the Power to Become 67

13. Start Living Today as Though Immortal 73

14. Cherish a Vision of Your Promised Land 77

15. Discover that Love is Stronger than Fear 81

16. Maintain a Forward Momentum 85

17. Always Face Eastward 89

18. Accept Responsibility for Yourself 95

19. Learn to Handle Life's Interruptions 101

20. Learn How to Throw Temptations Down the Stairs 107

21. Develop the Power of Perseverance 113

22. Deepen the Root of a Patient Spirit 117

23. Learn to Sing in Your Darkness 121
24. Will Yourself to Be Happy 127
25. Get Yourself Off Your Hands 131
26. Put More Holiness into Sex..............................137
27. Acquire Inward Peace by Wading Through.....................143
28. Learn to Live One Day at a Time.........................149
29. Accept the Interrelatedness of Prayer and Action.............153
30. Discover Your Need to Get Involved 159
31. Learn the Necessity of Holy Indignation 165
32. Accept the Inevitability of Suffering 171
33. Live as Though Divine Healing Is Likely 177
34. Cast the Dark Bogey Out of Dying 181
35. Count on Life After Death 187
Notes 192

Introduction

Grow in the grace and knowledge of our Lord and Savior Jesus Christ
(2 Pet. 3:18).

One evening a young mother heard a thump on the floor overhead. Hurrying upstairs, she found her five-year-old girl on the floor in a tangle of bedclothes. Picking her up, the mother asked anxiously, "Susie, are you all right?"

The child nodded sleepily.

"How did you happen to fall out of bed?"

There was silence for a moment, followed by a yawn. "I guess I went to sleep too close to where I got in!"

What a warning this can be for Jesus' disciples. Some of us may be new to the fellowship of Christ, having been attracted by a church program or an individual's urgent sense of evangelism. Others may have participated for years in religious activities and are growing into an enlarging faith. Still others of us have been blessed with a memorable experience of having been wrapped in God's mantle or of having been accepted into the living comradeship of Jesus, or however else we would describe a sudden experience of salvation.

Authentic faith is not necessarily a once-and-for-all-time attainment, but faith is a continuum of spiritual growth which begins at whatever level of experience we enter, demanding of us constant maturing up until the moment of death. How sad it is to see children baptized at an early age, then neglecting their faith in later years because they do not

7

understand that lifelong learning must mark their relation to God! And it is even sadder when adults, who have once committed themselves in some breathtaking experience, gradually slip into insensitivity because, contented with the memory of their initial glow, they have failed "to grow up in every way . . . into Christ" (Eph. 4:15). They have fallen asleep too close to where they got in!

Growth into spiritual maturity, therefore, is essential for every sincere disciple of Jesus. Many practical approaches can encourage growth into that maturity. This volume suggests thirty-five guidelines by which we can assume responsibility for such growth.

Its title comes from a conversation I once had with a woman beset by three small children and a husband overworked by his corporation. She remarked, "There's a lot of advice in books and magazines, on radio and TV, about 'How to Cope.' Some of it I've found to be helpful. But mostly it deals with secular stuff—how to unplug the sink and that sort of thing—while as a Christian, I should be able to do more than just manage. I need to get a little ahead of the game, to 'get a hammerlock on life,' as my husband would say. I need, well, guidelines which can lead me beyond just coping and into mastering my life!"

Isn't she right! When people of faith can barely cope and can't get that hammerlock on their daily living, don't they need assistance in growing in grace and in the knowledge of Christ? Since its inception, Christianity has provided guidelines for becoming "more than conquerors," with the result that countless millions have learned how to grow spiritually, saved from inconsequential, superficial existence by the enabling power of God.

But here a note of warning must be sounded about the use of any sort of religious gimmickry. We are saved from superficial, inconsequential existence not by "surefire techniques," however faithfully applied, but by the power of God made available to us through faith in Jesus. Guidelines are useful only when they reinforce this truth: "By grace you have been saved through faith; and this is not your own doing, it is the gift of God—not because of works, lest any man should boast" (Eph. 2:8-9). Since this is so, then why should anyone worry about growing into a larger faith? Why bother with the nuisance of conforming to guidelines such as those which follow?

The answer is twofold. First, when we care about the quality of our spiritual lives and do what lies within our power to become more like Jesus, *we give God the cooperation He needs in order to complete in us, through Jesus, His saving work.* Constantly, He is urging us toward complete self-surrender to Him. Thus, for us to accept spiritual discipline is evidence of our responsiveness. God does not do for us what we can do for ourselves. His saving grace is not effectual until we really want it—until we "hunger and thirst for righteousness" (Matt. 5:6). Our consuming desire *to grow into maximum holiness of thought and deed, under the stimulus of His urging, provides God with the opportunities He needs to do for us everything He wants to do.* And every way in which we can apply biblical teaching and religious inspiration to our daily living will bring us closer to Him. We cannot reach Him merely by our own efforts, of course; there come times when, in spite of our devotion, we "run out of steam." Then we discover that God comes to meet us with the resources of His enabling power and love. The Persian poet Firdusi wrote:

> Whoso draws nigh to God one step through doubtings dim,
> God will advance a mile in blazing light to him.

A second reason is that, for the fortunate person who has known the joy of a definite salvation experience and of growing up solidly within the household of faith, *spiritual growth must never stop.* Life in Christ is always beckoning us to new vistas, opening both to eternity and to our day-by-day living. Once we sense that we are accepted by God, drawn within His inner circle of loving concern, we may not settle down "in Harán" any more than Abram did. God has not completed His act of grace by saving us. His gathering of us into His love is but the beginning of a relation between Him and us, through the mediation of Jesus, which can become as rich as we allow Him to make it. God has intended this growth for us, and the acceptance of devotional guidelines may help us achieve it. Paul told the Ephesians, "We are his workmanship, created in Christ Jesus for good works, which God prepared beforehand, that we should walk in them" (Eph. 2:10). Therefore, whether we employ guidelines such as those which follow or develop our own, God stands ready to assist us in producing the practical "fruit of the Spirit" which indicate our growth.

Speaking the truth in love, we are to grow up in every way into him who is the head, into Christ (Eph. 4:15).

1.

Cling Boldly to the Fact that God Loves You

I have loved you with an everlasting love;
therefore I have continued my faithfulness to you (Jer. 31:3).

One of my early religious disillusionments was the discovery that an astonishingly large number of persons completely leave God out of their daily living. It may be they believe God has left them out of His calculations, and they are simply getting even with Him. "Just look at our world!" they exclaim. "Where is the evidence that God has any inkling of our plight?" They especially feel that He is absent from the international scene. They believe He is found neither in the surges of history nor in the thrust of contemporary events. Earthshaking catastrophes continually occur which threaten our hope for a better world, they charge, and yet, they claim, God gives no practical evidence of His love for humankind.

Or perhaps such antagonism has arisen out of personal troubles, since the sheen has suddenly been grated from their lives. Perhaps there was a lack of money, continued sickness, or unemployment. It may be that there were cruel disappointments, periods of loneliness or bereavement when God seemed to be utterly indifferent to their needs. It was easy, then, to cry, "God does not love me. I have to stand alone!"

Reasons for counting God out of our human experience may be summarized these three ways.

(1) *God is much too big to know about us.* That is, it is stupid to think that God would even be aware of such a sinful and fratricidal segment of His creation as human beings.

(2) *God simply does not care to get involved with humankind anymore.* He cannot be bothered with the triviality and junkiness of our modern life-style. He has 161 billion more important things to do in the next minute than trying to ride herd on such obstreperous creatures.

(3) *God actually is an absentee landlord Who simply is not around our earth often enough to be concerned about what we human beings are doing.* He cannot respond to our needs because when we want Him desperately, He is 543,000 light-years away, winding up a star which was beginning to loiter! God got everything started here, true enough, but He has now turned everything over to us "lock, stock, and barrel"! We are strictly on our own.

Now, how ridiculous! Claiming that *God is too big, too preoccupied, or too remote to be concerned about you and me!* Yet Scripture, tradition, and tested human experience testify that exactly the opposite is true. *Therefore, we may hold fast to three certainties.*

(1) *God Knows!* The fundamental, bedrock assumption on which all faith in God must ultimately rest is the certainty that God indeed does know about you and me, and knows all about us, even in embarrassing detail! "See what love the Father has given us," wrote John, "that we should be called children of God" (1 John 3:1). Unbelievably mighty a Creator though He be, He is at the same time breathlessly imminent, immediately available throughout His creation, "closer than breathing, nearer than hands and feet."

He is too big a God not to know! The unimaginably tremendous dimension of our Creator-Father causes Him to know what we are, what we do, and what happens to us. Whatever be your troubles or mine, whether they be backache, headache, or heartache—ills of body, mind, or spirit—we can face them confidently because God knows about them.

(2) *God cares!* Fortunately, the fact He *knows* is not the whole certainty we may have about God. Perhaps you have had some intensely personal and awesome experience when the veil between your soul and God's mighty Spirit was parted for a moment, and in wonder you discovered firsthand that you are known by God. When this happens, another basic conviction becomes at once apparent. You learn that *because God knows, He also cares!* "Cast all your anxieties on him, for he cares about you" (1 Pet. 5:7). Within our earthly existence, you and I are not always thus caring. How often my knowledge of something seriously wrong either with myself or my community does not spur me to care enough to do something about it! So, because such caring is not always characteristic of humankind, we tend to think that this also is not characteristic of God.

But He is too big not to care! He is too vast a reality to be occupied solely with maintaining the complex machinery of a trillion expanding universes! Because He knows that yesterday you or I let some inward defense against temptation crumble, He cared. Because He knows that today you or I may be facing some problem too great for our unaided strength, He cares. Because He knows that tomorrow the monotony of routine living may strip our spirits of their wings and turn us into dreary plodders, He cares.

(3) *God comes!* Even the above truths are not all we may know for certain about God. His knowing and caring about you and me by themselves are incomplete. For the climactic discovery which spiritual adventurers in every generation have made is that, knowing and caring about us, *God therefore comes to us.* "God will send from heaven and save me, he will put to shame those who trample upon me. God will send

forth his steadfast love and his faithfulness!" (Ps. 57:3). This we may prove in the same way those adventurers did—by putting it to the test in our daily living.

Once God came to us historically in the person of Jesus at the first Christmas, His mighty, enabling power being made flesh and dwelling among us, full of grace and truth. And God comes to us now, whenever we hunger for the divine relationship. There is only one qualification: "You will seek me and find me; when you seek me with all your heart, I will be found by you" (Jer. 29:13). God is no absentee landlord living in feudal isolation at some remote corner of His vast domain beyond the sound of our cries. He is much too big for that. Just for the very reason that He knows and cares, He comes to us in both our joy and sorrow, in our occasions of contentedness and distress.

Thus you and I have His continuing promise that when we are humiliated by failure and turn to Him, He will stir us up to make fresh attempts; when we are bitter over a friend's betrayal of our trust, He will draw the sting from our wounds and grant us a forgiving spirit; when we are prostrate over the death of one whom we have loved more than our own lives, He will restore us with conviction of life eternal for those who love Him.

On a visit to the English city of Coventry shortly after World War II, I talked with a man who had been a fire-warden during the obliteration bombings of 1940. He was on duty the night when Saint Michael's Cathedral, the love-ly thirteenth-century structure, was destroyed by fire-bombs.

"I was posted at Saint Mary's Street," he told me, "when a group of incendiaries caught the cathedral and put the roof in flames where we could not reach it. It was a terrible sight, and I felt that God had deserted us at the time of our greatest need. If the cathedral, which represented what was most precious in our heritage, could not be saved, of what use was it to fight for our homes?

"But as I stood by, full of despair at my helplessness to save the cathedral, I suddenly heard the sound of a bell. It was eleven o'clock, and the great clock in the tower of the doomed building was sending out its deep tones over the gutted city. I just can't describe the effect those bells on me and on other people that night. It was as though God had sensed the depth of our despair and was Himself standing within the flaming tower, beating out with His own hand the promise that even though the city were destroyed, there He was in our midst. And every hour throughout that hideous night, as the bell struck again and again, I remembered the old hymn by Adelaide A. Pollard:

> Fear not, I am with thee; O be not dismayed,
> For I am thy God, and will still give thee aid;
> I'll strengthen thee, help thee, and cause thee to stand,
> Upheld by my righteous, omnipotent hand.

"I tell you, my American friend," he said as we parted, "we went through hell that night and other nights. But God Himself walked with us!"

"As surely as God ever puts His children in the fiery furnace," exclaimed Charles Spurgeon, "He will be in the furnace with them."

Any God who does not know about you and me is a limited God Who is unqualified to be worshiped. Any God who does not care about us is a callous God, unworthy to be loved. Any God who does not come to us is an ineffectual God, unfit to be served. But our God, "who made the Pleiades and Orion" (Amos 5:8) puts aside His austere majesty and stoops to us in tender compassion and sustaining power.

Thus, the opening guideline for the mastery of life is to

accept joyously the fact that God knows about you and me, that He cares about us, and that He comes to us.

> He who does not love does not know God; for God is love. In this the love of God was made manifest among us, that God sent his only Son into the world, so that we might live through him (1 John 4:8-9).

2.

Locate a Place Where God and You May Meet

Hearken thou to the supplication of thy servant and of thy people . . . when they pray toward this place; yes, hear thou in heaven thy dwelling place; and when thou hearest, forgive (1 Kings 8:30).

Common to the world's ethical religions is this question, "Where can I find God?" Nearly sixteen-hundred years ago Saint Augustine wrote, "Thou hast made us for Thyself, and our souls are restless till they find rest in Thee!" He was not stating what would be nice to believe but was proclaiming the fundamental nature of human beings. You and I reach out for knowledge of God because He made us that way. We are programmed to search for Him because it is possible to find Him. We have known vague periods of restlessness, dissatisfaction with our present religious accomplishment, caused by what is eternal within us crying out after its Maker. Yet this stirring of the divine within us frequently is so indefinable that we cannot always know where to find its Source. At first, our relation to Him is remote and second-hand, till one time we hear His voice out of some suddenly sensed "burning bush," "Take off your shoes, for you are standing on holy ground!" To find such places of meeting is essential for the mastery of our daily living.

Since the dawn of history there have been descriptions of such places. Ancient peoples felt that some spirit was pulsing on every side, just out of sight of what they saw. Therefore they worshiped those objects in which resided a

seemingly mysterious power: the sun, twisted trees, curious
rocky outcrops, booming sea caverns, lightning flashes, and
the rest—places where they felt the deity could be most.

Centuries after the Hebrews had outgrown animistic ten-
dencies and were being prepared in the wilderness for invading Canaan, the special Place of Meeting became a thin
slab of gold covering a sacred casket known as the Ark of
God. This golden cover was the "mercy seat." "There," God
had told Moses, "I will meet with you" (Ex. 25:22). For
countless peoples today, the equivalent is their church's
altar or communion table—but there are other places of
meeting.

After the successful occupation of Canaan, the Place of
Meeting finally became the Holy of Holies in the inner sanc-
tum of the Jerusalem Temple, which endured till 70 AD.
And with Christianity came churches—groups of individuals voluntarily gathered for the worship of God—with the
assurance that where two or three hungering persons may be
found, there He is in their midst. Where better to find God
than in the company of those who earnestly seek Him? Does
not this belief keep people attending services of worship
even when their secular neighbors exclaim, "There are so
many more interesting things to do"?

But you and I cannot end our search here, or we will
neglect a resource which God specifically offered: "The
Word became flesh and dwelt among us, full of grace and
truth; we have beheld his glory, glory as of the only Son
from the Father" (John 1:14). Jesus is our Savior. He shows
us what God is like, what God wills for us, and He mediates
to us the forgiveness, the companionship, and the inspiration we need in order to achieve the divine purposes in our
everyday living. In Jesus the physical and spiritual worlds
meet; through Him the divine love is thrust into what is
human, and God becomes known to you and me as in no

other fashion. He is, indeed, the Way, for He says to us, "Come, I will take you to My Father!"

And our knowledge of Jesus reveals that there is a further Place of Meeting to be sought—deep within our own beings. For God "is not far from each one of us," declared Paul, and then quoting from Epimenides the Greek he added, " 'In Him we live and move and have our being' " (Acts 17:27-28). Everyone who has faithfully sought God through nature, through ark and Temple, through public worship, or through a vital fellowship with Jesus has by these means *transformed a bit of his or her own life into the sacred soil of a holy meeting place.* For God comes to you and me in the depths of our own spirits, directly, without intercessory aids. His Kingdom indeed can be within us! We do well to remember that for us, as for Elijah, the Lord is not in the whirlwind, the earthquake, or the fire but, rather, in a still, small, inward Voice.

Just as Sir Launfal's quest for the Holy Grail led back to the familiar scenes of home for its fulfillment, so also the search which you and I mount for the God to whom Jesus directs us, leads us finally back to the depths of our own being. We are to create within us an interior chapel and use it regularly in Jesus' spirit. In this ultimate Place of Meeting we shall be heartened to master our everyday living.

The eternal God is your dwelling place,/and underneath are the everlasting arms (Deut. 33:27).

3.

Convert Your Whole Life into One Holy Ground

God called to him out of the bush, "Moses, Moses!" And he said, "Here am I." Then he said, "Do not come near; put off your shoes from your feet, for the place on which you are standing is holy ground" (Ex. 3:4-5).

We must carry the "meeting place" one step further.

A small child once prayed, "Good-bye, God, we're moving to Chicago." This may have reflected the feeling which Moses had when he fled from Egypt to Midian, married a rancher's daughter, and settled down to the life of a sheepherder. For Midian was unhallowed ground, beyond the reach of the God to whom Moses was devoted. Psalm 139 had not yet been composed, nor the Book of Jonah, so Moses did not know at first that God was the Lord of the whole earth.

But one day as he herded the family flock near Mount Horeb, Moses was startled to see a bit of vegetation in flames. Alert to the danger of scrub fires which could destroy the all-too-thin grazing for his sheep, Moses ran up to check the fire. But he was halted abruptly by a voice of command, "Remove your sandals, for you are standing on holy ground!"

Holy ground? In Midian? To Moses the impossible had happened. Even though he was literally in the midst of "nowhere," under his bare feet was ground made holy by an authentic encounter with his God!

Here is an interesting phrase, "holy ground." As men-

tioned earlier, at one time it meant the space within the Holy
of Holies or the altars of great cathedrals. Today, however,
it usually refers to cemetery plots! And to the average person, no ground is holy!

Yet from Moses' experience, must we not conclude that
any spot where you and I sense the presence of God is holy? From his
experience we may make a fresh approach to our everyday
living. The particular place, of course, is not what is sacred,
so much as what goes on there between God and us. There
is no restriction, then, on the number of places in our lives
where we can suddenly realize we are standing on sacred
soil. The quality of our spiritual growth is marked by how
continuously you and I are able to enlarge the amount of
holy ground within us.

How sad it is that so many individuals, along with Ham-
let, find life to be "weary, flat, stale, and unprofitable," or
they agree with the Preacher, "Futility [vanity] of futilities!
All is futility!" It is tragic for them personally, and for the
society which must carry them as a deadweight. On those
rare occasions when I have momentarily been "down in the
dumps," it has happened by my temporarily misplacing my
"sense of the sacred." I have learned that when my awareness of God's overarching presence is dim, and when my
sense of companionship with Jesus is lost, the major source
of my joy, my purpose, and my self-realization is dammed
up. My resentments flourish like hardy weeds, my cynicism
surfaces, and my satisfactions turn to ashes.

Have you not known similar periods of "dryness," as the
mystics have termed them? Might they not stem from an
unrecognized dimming of our sense of the holiness invading
all our day-to-day living? Is not your need and mine the
recovery of the everyday companionship of the Almighty?
If so, then we may seek to enlarge the amount of holy
ground within us, praying, "Let the words of my mouth/and

the meditation of my heart/be acceptable in thy sight,/O Lord, my rock and my redeemer" (Ps. 19:14).

Here again, Jesus can be our Savior because He is a perfect example of the kind of life which God intends us to follow, and because He challenges us: "Walk in My Way, and I will take you to the furthest limits of your ability"—which may be further than we expect. The richness of His prayer life, for example, was a secret of His strength, yet He did not need to travel to His nation's holy places to pray. Wherever He stepped became a wayside shrine, and every bush was alive with the vibrant presence of His Father. He sensed continually the proximity of the sacred, and through it He practiced the presence of God.

Has He not thereby set an example for you and me? Every experience provides us with a similar opportunity for letting God command our days. This means that everything we do in the living room and kitchen, in recreation area and bedroom, as well as in the office, shop, or store, and in every outing and sporting event, offers opportunity for the same amazing experience which Moses had in his desolate wilderness. Whatever part of your life and mine is in particular use at any given moment can be transformed into holy ground because we have made God welcome there.

We grow into mature self-realization, then, as we steadily enlarge the areas of our lives which are under the sway of the Holy Spirit.

> Beloved, build yourselves up on your most holy faith; pray in the Holy Spirit; keep yourselves in the love of God; wait for the mercy of our Lord Jesus Christ unto eternal life (Jude 20:21).

4.
Continuously Orient Yourself Toward the Divine Light

The sun shall be no more your light by day,
nor for brightness shall the moon
give light to you by night;
but the Lord will be your everlasting light,
and your God will be your glory (Isa. 60:19).

One of the most effective ways you and I can increase the acreage given to holiness in our lives is continuously to respond to the Divine Light. We are constantly to keep facing toward the warmth of God's love, as a sunflower constantly turns its face to the sun. Many early peoples observed that certain plants such as the heliotrope made involuntary movements to keep their blossoms in sunshine. No one then understood the process but recognized that the sun was the source of the power which turned the blossoms.

But more than the sun exerts this power. This ability to turn toward light is found also within us and makes friendships possible. Your ability and mine to respond to the charm, the winsomeness, and the character of other individuals is the reason we make friends. Automatically, we turn to those who spread warmth and light about us. There is also a mutual turning toward each other by which a man and a woman, ensnared by each other's outgoing affection, fall in love and become life partners.

And indeed, the Four Gospels are demonstrations of the light which was and is in Jesus, attracting people to Him as

the sun attracts flowers. The rich and the poor, the sick and
the healthy, the affluent and the dispossessed are all por-
trayed as being magnetically drawn to the Master as a compass needle points north. And Jesus did not lose this power
at death. For the written records of His life have had power
to invoke from those who read them the same devotion
given by those who knew Him in the flesh. And they have
been led from Scriptural knowledge to direct, spiritual
awareness of the risen Christ.

But we must not stop here, because Jesus did not. He was
Himself impelled to acknowledge His Father. His compelling attractiveness lay primarily in the fact that the whole set
of His life was toward His Father, being completely attuned
to God's purposes. Because of this, *as we turn toward Jesus, we,
too, come face-to-face with God.* The psalmist exclaimed, "With
thee is the fountain of life;/in thy light do we see light (Ps.
36:9). Just so! We are so designed that we can communicate
with Him; we are tuned to one of His wavelengths. Something there is within your life and mine which turns us,
consciously or unconsciously, toward the Almighty. The
"Hymn of Joy" summarizes it perfectly: "Hearts unfold like
flowers before Thee, Praising Thee their sun above." This
kind of spontaneous turning to the Father is the most significant of all kinds.

Now, you and I can deny this aspect of our nature because
it appears to be unsuited to life in the computer age. "Scien-
tific humanity" is the new "sun" toward which we are invit-
ed to bow, unless it is toward television's newest "star" who
is rising above the horizon. Yet as humankind has turned to
such substitute suns, how often have they proved only to be
sky-rockets, beautiful to watch in their ascending and their
bursting, but burning out suddenly and falling to earth as
scorched and empty shells!

> For though they pierced the dark,
> They didn't hold back the night—
> In them was a transient spark,
> And not the Eternal Light.[1]

Then perhaps one day, in our carefree pace through everyday living, either you or I run headlong into a stone wall which looms suddenly across our path, or someone whom we love deeply is taken from us. As we try to pull our shattered bits together into some semblance of meaning, we become aware that we are turning, as bewildered children seek their parents, to the Source from which all meaning flows. Or when we are ashamed of some thoughtless word or sinful deed and instinctively hide our faces, by an act of will we can let the light-seeking power of our souls turn us again to God's presence. "If we walk in the light, as he is in the light, we have fellowship with one another, and the blood of Jesus his Son cleanses us from all sin" (1 John 1:7). Instinctively, becoming as sunflowers, we discover afresh the spiritual resources of our God-centeredness.

This power, therefore, is the basic design of our beings. Whereas the sunflower can turn toward the sun only during daylight hours, you and I are more fortunate. In the very blackest midnights we can turn to God, for "God is light, and in him is no darkness at all" (1 John 1:5).

Exactly! Our lives move toward their richest fulfillment when we respond to our inner impulses, as directed by the Holy Spirit, and joyously keep ourselves within the full radiance of the Divine Light.

> The Lord is my light and my salvation;
> whom shall I fear?
> The Lord is the stronghold of my life;
> of whom shall I be afraid? (Ps. 27:1).

5.

Let God Become an Occupying Power

May the God of hope fill you with all joy and peace in believing, so that by the power of the Holy Spirit you may abound in hope. (Rom. 15:13).

Yet another way in which you and I can increase the acreage given to holiness in our lives is to let God become an occupying Power within us.

How do you think of God, and how does that thought shape your relation to Him? Although the classic description underscored by Jesus is "your Father who is in heaven," not everyone thinks of Him in this fashion. Yet how we actually do regard Him predetermines our initial relationship. A wide variety of attitudes are taken toward God, of which four stand out.

(1) Some people think of Him as a *well-intentioned but ineffectual sort of Heavenly Grandfather, who was quite some person in His day, but whose age is finally catching up with Him.* A character in a current novel dismisses God with the offhand statement, "A harmless old gent with a Jehovah complex." And a college girl who had been upset by a number of visits to the Dean exclaimed, "God's a nice old guy, but not very helpful in an emergency!"

(2) Almost the opposite belief is held by those who announce that *God's major usefulness is in time of crisis.* Most elevators contain a button marked "Emergency" which can be pushed under dire circumstances. Now, to some individuals,

God is help they can summon in crisis. They get along
beautifully by themselves much of the time, but when trouble suddenly rears up, they speed to the fire-alarm box, as
it were, jerk down the lever, and expect the divine fire en-
gines to start rolling! Or to change the metaphor, God is a
Copilot who can take over the controls when they slip from
our nerveless hands.

(3) Others see God as *a Serviceman or Troubleshooter whom we
can call in to repair some part of our lives which has gotten out of
adjustment.* Or He is like a watchmaker to whom we take our
complex lives for an occasional cleaning or regulating, or else
a dentist whom we should visit regularly every six months—
or perhaps at Christmas and Easter!—for spiritual pro-
phylaxis and the filling of our soul's cavities.

Now, persons who think of God primarily as an emergency lever, as a Service Repairman or as a Copilot, honestly
believe they are exalting God. They intend to honor Him by
thus admitting Him to a position of occasional usefulness in
their lives. *But what a comedown that is for God!* For He is being
reduced from "Lord of all being, throned afar, whose glory
flames from sun and star" to what Dean Shailer Matthews
termed "a cosmic bellhop!" Such attitudes toward God fall
short because they put "me" at life's center as controller and
director and put God as a Special First Assistant in Charge
of Emergencies! Thus, the distinguishing mark of my attitude toward God is not one of humbleness but of conde-
scension.

(4) If God is not to be thought of as an emergency switch,
a Troubleshooter, or a Cosmic Bellhop, what relation to you
and me does He most greatly desire? And which, therefore,
will be most wholesome for us? How about considering that
He is to be an Occupying Power in your life?

From 1946 to 1959 Germany was occupied fully by the

military forces of the four Allied victors. To ensure the rooting out of the foul disease of Nazism, England, France, and the United States moved into every nook and cranny of Germany's economic, social, political, and educational life. An all-out effort was made by three of the four powers in West Germany to create a new order based on fundamental democratic and Christian principles. And in the more than twenty-five years that the Bonn government has been on its own, we have witnessed two miracles: one, the amazing economic recovery, and the other, the equally amazing manner in which that whole nation, never having had a genuine experience of democracy in its hundreds of years of history, has grasped and adopted Western political principles. With the possible exception of America's occupation of Japan, the world has never seen a more dramatically creative result of military occupation.

Now, may not this instance serve as a parable of God's relation to us? For through Jesus, I learn that *God wants to be an Occupying Force in my life, requiring the submission of my sinful spirit to the Divine Will, which directs me into the patterns of living which He intends me to follow.* To yield myself to His commanding control is the whole purpose of authentic religious living. "You are not in the flesh," wrote Paul, "you are in the Spirit, if in fact the Spirit of God really dwells in you" (Rom. 8:9). Yet, unlike the commander of a victorious army, God does not storm the redoubt of my ego, forcing Himself on me willy-nilly; rather, He awaits my invitation. And how often, instead of welcoming Him, I start a "resistance movement" which will guard and protect my desire to continue being just whatever I choose to be! Oh, God is all right as an emergency button or a Copilot but not as an Occupying Power, a High Commissioner whose word is absolute law! On occasion I sing:

Have thine own way, Lord! Have thine own way!
Thou art the Potter, I am the clay!
Mold me and make me After thy will,
While I am waiting, Yielded and still.[2]

But how often do I really mean it?

Yet, when you and I welcome the holy invasion, we take an essential step toward mature living. For when we fling wide our lives to God, not as a Heavenly Grandfather or Cosmic Bellhop, but as the Creator and Inspirer of our little selves, we fulfill the role God has chosen for us. Our self-centered patterns of living may be shattered into a thousand pieces, but God will reassemble those fragments into new patterns more like that of Jesus. "All who keep his commandments abide in him, and he in them" (1 John 3:24).

In his biography of Woodrow Wilson, Ray Stannard Baker relates how the president unexpectedly visited his alma mater, Davidson College, and out of curiosity went unannounced to his old room, number 13, in Chambers Hall. Hoping to see what it looked like after the passage of years, he knocked on the door. The freshman within was reading in a rocking-chair and called out, "Who's there?"

"Woodrow Wilson," came the reply.

"OK," sang out the student, "you've got nothing on me. Come on in. I'm Christopher Columbus!"

But when the student glimpsed who his visitor actually was, he gave the president an agonizing look and went right out the window, leaving only an empty chair rocking back and forth to greet the president.

The Divine Occupying Force is always at your door and mine. As John recorded it, "Behold, I stand at the door and knock; if anyone hears my voice and opens the door, I will come in to him and eat with him, and he with me" (Rev. 3:20). How are we to greet Him? Do we flee in panic? Sometimes we may. Do we lock the door and prepare for a siege? Sometimes we may.

Yet we will grow in spiritual maturity as we let God become an Occupying Power in our lives.

All who are led by the Spirit of God are sons of God (Rom. 8:14).

6.

Rejoice in God's Providence

The Lord redeems the life of his servants; none of those who take refuge in him will be condemned (Ps. 24:32).

Shortly after World War II, I picked up a hitchhiker who had been a paratrooper sergeant. He told me how once, in a scramble to board their transport plane, his parachute was accidentally swapped for another trooper's, and when they jumped, his parachute, worn by the other man, failed to open.

"How could that have happened?" I asked.

He shrugged. "Joe's number was up. It was his turn not to make it. Fate had to step in and make the swap, because it wasn't my turn."

As we talked further, he said, "The universe rolls around me, not giving a — even while automatically protecting me. Then, when my number comes up, the universe simply shifts gears like a gigantic slot machine and rolls over me, still not giving a —."

A similar sense of fatalism has usually been found among armed forces in wartime, and some of it has carried over into our present day, even without the pressures of deadly combat which shaped so much thinking during the war years. Yet fatalism is totally alien to Christian belief. It is a superficial way to deal with crises, blaming everything—including the careless packing of a parachute—on "how the stars were stacked" at one's birth. It presupposes cosmic caprice, an intergalactic lottery.

Thus the universe is believed to be totally without intelligent and compassionate supervision. At my birth, that is, I was stamped with whatever fate results from that moment's particular conjunction of stars and planets, and this fate is unalterable. Neither I nor anyone else has the power to effect any change in what has been predetermined for me, according to this view. Not only does this relieve me from any sense of responsibility for what happens to me, or anyone else, and robs me of my essential dignity—which is fatal to my character-growth—but it also portrays God as a useless figurehead unable to countermand the inflexible pattern of events in which I am hopelessly entrapped.

By contrast, what is the insight of Jesus? Well, there is an old-fashioned word in religious vocabularies which has almost disappeared from modern usage, but it describes Jesus' belief. It is the word *Providence,* meaning God's overarching provision for His children's needs—a concept which is essential to our faith. When we speak of Providence, we mean the particularized, loving care exercised by God over the entire universe. The word is derived from the Latin *pro* and *videre* meaning "forward looking." God exercises foresight on our behalf, making provision in advance for our wants. His love surrounds us; His care upholds us.

One of the most corrosive feelings you and I could have is that of facing the vast, still unknown universe all alone. The minute we feel that God is absent from the world, replaced by a heartless machine which grinds us up like Johnny Verbeck's machine, we slip down like John Bunyan's Pilgrim into a "slough of despond." Because there is no sensible alternative, we may struggle bravely to climb out of the slough unassisted. But without supporting belief in God, we tend to slide back down again.

Yet there is no good reason for this to happen. Do you know this poem by Elizabeth Cheney?

> Said the robin to the Sparrow:
>   "I should really like to know
> Why these anxious human beings
>   Rush around and scurry so."
> Said the Sparrow to the Robin:
>   "Friend, I think that it must be
> That they have no Heavenly Father
>   Such as cares for you and me."

But that answer is for the birds! We do have a loving, caring, coming Father who watches over us. It pays to explore the meaning of these phrases of Jesus: "Take no thought" (KJV), "Do not be anxious," "Your heavenly Father knows" (Matt. 6:25-31). As you and I put God's loving Providence to the test, depending each day on His personal concern for us, what burdens may be lifted from us!

Thus fatalism is only a pale, insubstantial shadow against the full-bodied reality of God's Providence. Fatalism is a product of ignorance, not of understanding; of crisis, not of quiet faith; of relinquishing control over life, not of acquiring more effective control. Fatalism is the result of a mechanistic interpretation of God's universe, demanding cosmic manipulations which play favorites capriciously in defiance of universal laws. By contrast, Providence declares that "in everything God works for good with those who love him, who are called according to his purpose" (Rom. 8:28). Fatalism is a soulless jester jerking puppet strings. Providence is a Father providing for His children. And He has an "answering service," about which I have written this poem.

> I do not need to build an Ark
>   To weather storm or shock:

> For when I pray through storm and dark,
> God sends one to my dock.

As I accept what Jesus taught, I will have no room for
fatalism because I will have an absolute, unwavering confidence in the love and care of God. When I give myself into
His keeping, all things—including sorrow, disappointment,
and bereavement—enrich my life, because God has struc-
tured the universe that way.

Rufus Jones has contrasted two bathers at a beach. One
thrashes around wildly in the water, trying to lift as much
of his body out as possible. To him, water is *something which
pulls him down in order to drown him!* The other bather, however,
coasts blissfully around on his back with only two toes and
a nose showing. To him water is *a friendly object which buoys him
up!*

Is not this a useful parable? Do you believe that the universe is devoid of meaning and love, that it is pulling you
down, overwhelming you so that life is one constant thrashing around to escape being drowned? Rather, are you not
confident that within and through all of life there "standeth
God within the shadow, keeping watch above his own"?

You and I will grow in spiritual maturity as we rejoice in
God's effectual Providence.

> Thou dost keep him in perfect peace,
> whose mind is stayed on thee,
> because he trusts in thee.
> Trust in the Lord forever,
> for the Lord God
> is an everlasting rock (Isa. 26:3-4).

7.

Rediscover the Historic Jesus

But when the time had fully come, God sent forth his Son, born of woman, born under the law, to redeem those who were born under the law, so that we might receive adoption as sons (Gal. 4:4).

Although several hundred years separate the latest-written book of the Old Testament from the earliest-written book of the New Testament, that gap is bridged securely at both ends. First there is God's promise, made through Jeremiah: "The days are coming, . . . when I will make a new covenant with the house of Israel and the house of Judah, . . . I will put my law within them, and I will write it upon their hearts" (Jer. 31:31-33). Then there is the opening proclamation of Hebrews: "In many and various ways God spoke of old to our fathers by the prophets; but in these last days he has spoken to us by a Son, . . . He reflects the glory of God and bears the very stamp of his nature" (Heb. 1:1-3).

The instrument God chose for fulfilling Jeremiah's prophecy was Jesus. We are to learn, therefore, as much about the historic Jesus as possible, so we may understand more fully how He fulfils the divine purpose and how we ourselves may be fulfilled through Him.

The promise was redeemed, however, in an unexpected manner, launched with no worldwide fanfare of publicity, in the birth of a baby within an obscure corner of the Roman Empire. Of this Son's childhood we know little. Joseph, His earthly guardian, was of the working class, and no doubt the boy learned the carpenter's trade. It is likely that at Joseph's death the young man assumed the support of His family. For years He lived quietly in Nazareth, not marrying, and at about the age of thirty He entered public life. Discontented with the spiritual life of His people and imbued with a sense of divine calling which flowed from His remarkably close relation with God, He began to preach a new and amazing doctrine. A person can be saved to holier living and be forgiven of sins, He declared, not by punctilious observance of more than six-hundred injunctions within Moses' law, nor by any system of ceremonial purification, but only by establishing through Jesus a direct, spiritual relation to God.

This new teacher was called the wildest of radicals, and before three years were past the respected religious establishment had accomplished His arrest, trial, and execution as a criminal. Yet within three centuries after His crucifixion, history had been redated with reference to his birth, men and women had died by the thousands in widespread persecution, so as to be counted His faithful disciples. And a new force—the spirit of lovingkindness—had begun to influence human decisions.

In spite of this, there are persons today who deny that such a person as Jesus ever lived. They point to the fact that the New Testament is the only original record of His life and declare that He is but a fanciful myth devised by scheming individuals for their own selfish purposes. One such disbeliever wrote a twelve-hundred-page manuscript "proving" that Jesus never had lived, and for endorsement he sent it to the Hebrew Union College in Cincinnati. There Dr. Benjamin Cohen wrote a scathing rejection of the manuscript, declaring that no person of sober scholastic instincts could doubt that Jesus actually lived.

The alleged "silence of history" about Jesus has not prevented eight-hundred-million persons today from proclaiming their faith in Him. From what they have read in the New Testament, from the record of tradition, from what they have seen in the sweep of world events since Jesus' day, and from what they have learned through their own experience, they exclaim with Whittier:

> The healing of His seamless dress
> Is by our beds of pain;
> We touch Him in life's throng and press,
> And we are whole again.

Why should this be so? Here is what J. S. Hutton said: "Once in the long course of history the sheer light and truth of God reached us by a medium so pure, so clear, so free from any inner distress or contamination or failure that it was white as the light itself; and men saw God in Christ." And in taking that Light to ourselves, we are saved to new usefulness in life. Here is the heart and soul of our faith: the miracle of the incarnation, which is the coming of the living Son of God—in the flesh—into a dark and sinful world, to be our Savior and Friend.

You and I may accept this miracle because human experience in every generation has proved that Jesus' life, spent in a tough time in history, is the holiest pattern by which to shape our lives: a pattern as viable as when He walked the earth. Possessing the nature of God, He rested His whole life on foundations which God Himself had laid. In Eugenia Price's words, he held "all that could be contained of God in a human being." This is a modern echo of Paul's insight: "Christ embodies all the fulness of God's nature" (Col. 2:9, VV). We recognize Him to be the human face of the Almighty. As a child once expressed it, "Jesus is the best photograph which God ever took of Himself." And this, also, is a restatement of the verse: "[Christ] is the image of the invisible God" (Col. 1:15). Our Master's knowledge of

what is durable, real, and eternal caused Him to proclaim
rock-bottom spiritual facts about life and its Creator. He
encompassed the entire realm of life, and with courage He
based His daily living on His revolutionary insights.

The result was that He lived completely in harmony with
the spiritual laws of the universe, even when this earned
Him the enmity of the religious establishment. His enor-
mous courage came from the knowledge that the Father and
the entire universe were on His side. So at one was He with
God and all creation, so fully surrendered to the divine will,
that the purpose of God shone through Him with clarity and
compelling persuasiveness. He was "white as the light itself," or as we sing at Christmas, "God with man is now
residing."

Just what was God's purpose, of which the Incarnation
was the initial phase? Paul stated it memorably:

> God has allowed us to know the secret of his plan, and it is
> this: he purposed long ago in his sovereign will that all
> human history should be consummated in Christ, that ev-
> erything that exists in Heaven or earth shall find its perfec-
> tion and fulfilment in him. And here is the staggering thing:
> in all which will one day belong to Him, we have been given
> an inheritance, . . . So that we, in due time, as the first to put
> our hope in Christ, may bring praise to his glory! (Eph. 1:9-
> 12, Phillips).

Jesus' earthly part in this plan was both to make it known
to people and win their acceptance of it through His teaching and example, and through His resurrection and continuing companionship. To believe in Him, therefore, is to accept
the grace which God offers to humankind. For "in Christ
God was reconciling the world to himself" (2 Cor. 5:19).

Thus in accepting Jesus in His fullest dimension as found
in the New Testament, instinctively we will test our lives by

His. Disturbed by the consequent discovery of our own life's pitiable dimensions, we will be led to cry, "Lord, I believe; help thou my unbelief!" In His own life Jesus marked the path which we may take to God's nearer presence. Peter put it this way: "Christ also suffered for you, leaving you an example, that you should follow in his steps" (1 Pet. 2:21).

Two men were discussing religion when one commented in exasperation, "If God really loves us, as you say, why doesn't He come down and tell us face to face?"

The other replied simply, "He did!"

You and I, therefore, will mature spiritually as we probe the deeper meanings of the Incarnation and the recorded details of Jesus' life.

> In [Jesus] all the fulness of God was pleased to dwell, and through him to reconcile to himself all things (Col. 1:19-20).

8.

Rediscover the Contemporary Jesus

If anyone is in Christ, he is a new creation; the old has passed away, behold, the new has come. . . . So we are ambassadors for Christ, God making his appeal through us (2 Cor. 5:17-20).

In addition to those persons who deny that Jesus ever lived, there are those who treat Him as no more than an historical phenomenon whose vital impact occurred two thousand years ago. They invest Jesus with a patina of antiquity, so that what He said and did is not relevant to our modern times but is of interest only to religious archaeologists and ecclesiastical historians. Such persons regard Jesus simply as another Socrates, a good man long dead, who might have helped us had we lived in His generation, who is still interesting to study but who has little to offer to the closing decades of the twentieth century.

You and I, then, may need to recognize how subtle a temptation it is to regard Jesus as being *only historical in nature, not contemporaneous;* to link him to biblical anthropology; to deny that He has the right to make demands on us today; to believe that His teachings and examples are outmoded and, as the inevitable result, to allow Jesus to exert negligible impact on our lives. This danger is epitomized by the comment of a county politician, "Aw, Christ's been dead for better'n nineteen-hundred years. Don't let's try to solve our problems with dead ghosts!" Or as an unnamed writer put it: "Jesus shut within a book/Does not get a passing look!"

But the Incarnate Good News of God is not clothed in the musty garments of antiquity! In our quest for spiritual maturity, do not you and I most need the certainty that Jesus is not merely an historic figure of the first century, but He is *"our Eternal Contemporary"?* He was also speaking to us of the closing decades of this century when He beckoned, "Take my yoke upon you, and learn from me; for I am gentle and lowly in heart, and you will find rest for your souls" (Matt. 11:29). Note that Jesus said, "I am," not "I was"! Ever since the first Easter, the Jesus of history has been the contemporaneous Christ, who treads our city streets just as surely as He trod the dusty paths of Palestine. This is where we must learn to find Him—"where cross the crowded ways of life," perhaps right on the block where we live—recognizing that His saving work goes on all around us. Just what is that saving power which the contemporary Jesus offers us? The British religious philosopher, Josiah Royce, has given us this description: "To find real forgiveness, to know the strange power of a love that will not let us go, to know a new sense of cleanness within—this is what it means to be saved; to be saved from all that separation from God means." Hebrews drives this miracle home: "[Jesus] is able for all time to save those who draw near to God through him" (Heb. 7:25). To be forgiven, loved, and cleansed—what more could we ask?

Yet sometimes individuals have deliberately locked Jesus back in the New Testament, in the hope of preventing Him from interfering with matters as they are now. How often He has been entombed in history, across whose door has been rolled the stone of tradition, ridicule, or defiance, so as to forestall any unwanted resurrection! Today, anyone who wants to run things to suit himself must first eliminate the influence of Jesus who continually proclaims God's sovereignty over all existence. Samuel Butler once opined, "There will be no comfortable and safe development of our social arrangements—I mean that we shall not get infanticide, nor the permission for suicide, nor cheap and easy divorce—till Jesus Christ's ghost has been laid!" And one way to lay His ghost is to keep Him shrouded in the mummy case of history.

Observing the contemporary scene, Herman Reissig once exclaimed, "I am forced to the conclusion that we are afraid of Jesus. The simple fact is that to take Jesus seriously calls for a revolution in our whole manner of life." Down deep, I know that I do not want to be the victim of a revolution! *"We refuse to face Jesus in our social relationships,"* Dr. Reissig continued, *"for the same reason that his contemporaries crucified him— not because they did not understand him, but because they did!"*

How serious a temptation is this to you and me? How real, immediate, and intimate a personality is the Master to us? When someone calls the name "Jesus," do we find ourselves suddenly transported back to the year AD 26 wherein we picture a strong-featured, neatly-bearded man clad in flowing white robes, at home in the "dear dead days beyond recall"? Or does His resurrection mean enough to us so that when we hear His name, our hearts and minds suddenly kindle with deep warmth? Is He an unseen but real Friend who walks with us as often as we will let Him, guiding and blessing our daily living? For if we will, we can see in Him today *"God's power working for the redemption of all who believe"* (Rom. 1:16, VV).

A fledgling missionary once confessed his initial failure, when on his second day on the foreign field an elderly native asked him, "Sir, tell me about Jesus."

Delighted, the young man began, "Well, He was born in Bethlehem about the year 6 BC. His father was a carpenter. When He was twelve . . ."

His listener interrupted politely. "I am acquainted with

the historic facts. Now please tell me what Jesus means to you." He wanted an introduction to the Contemporaneous Christ!

Later, when relating this humiliation, the missionary said, "Only then did I realize that my values had been in reverse. My first thought of Jesus had been historical. I learned then that it should be totally different. *The risen Lord who walks with me to all my Emmauses comes first; the historic foundations are secondary.*"

Contrast this young man's first experience with that of Helen Keller who, on a visit to Kobe College in Japan, was asked the identical question: "What does Jesus mean to you?"

When this was relayed to Miss Keller, a radiant smile touched her face. "Jesus is my light," she exclaimed, "and the harmony of my life." To that blind and deaf woman, this was all the light and harmony she had, but it was enough! To her Jesus was, in Whittier's lines,

> No fable old, nor mythic lore,
> > No dreams of bards and seers,
> No dead fact stranded on the shore
> > Of the oblivious years—

> But warm, sweet, tender, even yet
> > A present help is He;
> And faith has still its Olivet,
> > And love its Galilee.

It was this contemporary Jesus who inspired Paul to exult, "I can do all things in him who strengthens me" (Phil. 4:13). And this strength is available to us today.

In his novel *The Brothers Karamazov*, Dostoevsky described how Jesus returned to earth to preach the gospel once again, choosing this time the streets of Seville in Spain. At once the

Grand Inquisitor had Him arrested, and in the dead of night goes to the prison to interrogate Him.

"Why have you come back?" he growls forbiddingly. "You left your task to the Church, and we know much better how to fulfill it in this world than You did. Go, and never come again!" That is, hurry back into that dead past where you will trouble us no more!

You and I grow in faith as we continually make sure that for us, *Jesus is not interred in the tomb of history or limited to the boundaries of first-century geography.* Rather, let it be that, as Thomas C. Clark has written:

> Our faith is in the Christ who walks
> With men today in street and mart;
> The constant Friend who thinks and talks
> With those who seek him in the heart.

For we have Jesus' promise, "Lo, I am with you always, to the close of the age" (Matt. 28:20).

A tourist hiking along a back road in the Kander valley of Switzerland paused to ask a little goatherd, "Where is the Breithorn? I would like to climb it if I could find the trail."

The lad replied, "I've never been there, Sir. But up there, beyond that waterfall, is the trail; and I know that my older brother would be glad to guide you."

Neither you nor I know what Breithorn or Jungfrau of aspiration our life's journey one day will take us. But through reading and rereading the Gospels and Epistles, we may confidently assert, "Here is the road, the highway of gentleness and teachableness, of obedience, integrity, and courage on which God has placed our feet. And here is Jesus, our Elder Brother, who will guide us."

You and I, therefore, will mature spiritually as we rediscover the continuing companionship of the contemporary Jesus.

For [God] has made known to us in all wisdom and insight
the mystery of his will, according to his purposes which he
set forth in Christ as a plan for the fulness of time, to unite
all things in him (Eph. 1:9-10).

9.

Utilize the Divine Chemistry of the Cross

For the sake of Christ, then, I am content with weaknesses, insults, hardships, persecutions, and calamities; for when I am weak, then I am strong (2 Cor. 12:10).

How would you like to invent a manufacturing process which could change a two-dollar bar of iron into a ninety-thousand-dollar bar of gold? How would you like to create a magic talisman which, when placed on a diseased area, would cure it? How would you like to discover an elixir so potent that a spoonful would restore lost youth?

Such creations have not yet appeared, although not for the lack of human effort! During the Middle Ages many persons devoted their lives to the study of alchemy, and although the groundwork was thereby laid for the sciences of chemistry and pharmacology, the attempt to find a sovereign "philosopher's stone" never succeeded.

In my childhood, sometimes I daydreamed about possessing a magical power which would enable me to take unheard-of shortcuts to my desires. For example, I would visualize myself being called from the baseball field at Roosevelt Junior High School directly to the pitcher's mound in Chicago's Wrigley Field, for a full season of big-league shutouts and three perfect games. A friend once disclosed that he would sometimes stop in the middle of an A-scale finger exercise to savor the vision of suddenly astounding his music teacher by carelessly switching to Rach-maninoff's "Second Piano Concerto."

Indeed, this habit isn't confined to childhood, for even in our adult years don't you and I find ourselves yearning to solve in one fell swoop all the problems which trouble us and everyone else? Don't we at times hunger for a philoso-pher's stone which can turn our ordinary, often mediocre living into golden self-fulfillment! Yet we shrug our shoul-ders because it seems impossible that the base metals of our everyday existence could ever be transmuted into the pre-cious metals of Christlike living. At one time or another, haven't we longed for the direct action of God in our affairs!

Through the Passion accounts, the New Testament indi-cates that this was also true of Jesus. A temptation which occurred throughout His ministry was to utilize the miracu-lous power of God as a shortcut, enabling Him to accomplish spectacularly the difficult tasks committed to Him. And dur-ing His agony on the cross, when all His work seemed to have been in vain, when public humiliation was a heavy burden, and when life itself was ebbing away, He cried out, "My God, why?" Why? Why didn't God intervene with a miracle and take from Jesus the pain of defeat, shame, and death?

The answer, of course, is that this is exactly what God did, not in the way we might have chosen but in His own way. Didn't He shape a stupendous miracle around Calvary? Al-chemy may not be possible in the physical world, but it is part of God's plan in the realm of Spirit, to enable you and me to grow in grace. For it is obvious that a divine chemistry had been at work over that darkened weekend, transmuting the cross from wood into gold, as it were, changing it from an object of torture, shame, and defeat into a symbol of power and victory!

Although this happened to Jesus on Easter morning, it

does indeed directly involve you and me. Here is not an isolated miracle passed just once by God on behalf of His beloved Son and then laid carefully away in mothballs. *Rather, it is a basic principle of the cosmos, built into the spiritual universe in which we dwell.* The principle of alchemy, unavailable in the material world, does operate within the realm of Spirit. It can change lives darkened by mistake, failure, or tough "luck" into lives bright with hope and joy. Thus, what occurred on Easter is not only a single historic event which happened to Jesus, which we remember annually, *but rather, a continuous occurrence among His modern disciples.* The divine Alchemy can turn our Good Fridays into Easters, too! "Thanks be to God," exulted Paul, "who gives us the victory through our Lord Jesus Christ" (1 Cor. 15:57).

Let us examine specifically one area where this principle operates today. Joseph Fort Newton once declared that public enemy number one is not fear but loneliness, which in turn fathers all sorts of anxieties and fears. Consider those individuals who have lived well into the twilight years, who have outgrown their sense of being needed, overdrawn their physical strength, reduced their financial resources, outlived their closest friends, and lost the concern of their loved ones. Just when life should be offering them a lovely sunset with a quiet afterglow, the hour has become dark and forbidding. They feel shut out from life, love, and hope. Or again, there are people who are "shut-in," victims of shyness, of utter lack of self-confidence, imprisoned in themselves by their own doubts and fears. Like trap-door spiders, they have gone underground and pulled the door fast behind them, and corrosive loneliness begins eating them up.

Thus, there are present in life many malignant powers which, when they gain the upper hand, can send human souls crashing down to defeat. *But followers of Jesus have access to a greater power than these, to which you and I may turn in confidence.*

For the best evidence of the alchemy principle is not just in the Gospels but also in everyday events, wherein you and I learn through our own experience that God's power can change our darkest Good Fridays into golden dawns of Easter victories.

Thus we mature in spirit as we utilize the Divine Alchemy of the cross.

Whatever is born of God overcomes the world; and this is the victory that overcomes the world, our faith. Who is it that overcomes the world but he who believes that Jesus is the Son of God! (1 John 5:4-5).

10.
Put on the Insignia
of Jesus

Let the word of Christ dwell in you richly, teach and admonish one another in all wisdom, and sing psalms and hymns and spiritual songs with thankfulness in your hearts to God. And whatever you do, in word or deed, do everything in the name of the Lord Jesus, giving thanks to God the Father through him (Col. 3:16-17).

The finger ring may be the earliest form of insignia, for signet rings have been unearthed in Egyptian tombs of the fifteenth century BC. From such simple beginnings the use of insignia has grown until most every organization, big or little, good or evil, maintains a cluster of emblems and logos it recognizes as distinctively its own. There is a variety of values in the use of such insignia.

(1) One reason is that when I wear a particular emblem, *it serves as a public acknowledgement of my relation to a particular group.* In letting it be seen, I am stating I belong to that organization and believe in what it stands for. Its concerns are my concerns; its ideals, my ideals; its convictions, my convictions; and even its failures, my failures.

Similarly, I find satisfaction in putting myself squarely on the record, declaring that I insist on being counted in matters being dealt with by my group. By wearing an emblem I serve notice that I wish to be known and judged even as my organization is known and judged.

And in wearing an insignia of a group which is admired in society, I claim such admiration for myself. Because that group enjoys community respect, I share in its regard. Certain excellence, that I may not yet possess, flows out of the group into me; I take on stature from that affiliation which might not have been gained were I not a member. With most people this is a value to "belonging," for the loftier purposes of insignia are quite different from that of my reaping a personal benefit from using them.

(2) A second value is that *insignia affords personal identification to members of the same organization who may be strangers to one another.* Emblems perform introductions for people of different neighborhoods, cities, regions, and even nations. To recognize on a stranger the same emblem I wear is immediately to think, *That person is a brother, or sister! We must get acquainted.*

On many occasions when I have been far from home, my car has broken down. Even though the city and the state have been unfamiliar, I have always headed directly for a church parsonage. The minister I have located sometimes has belonged to a different denomination from mine and has never laid eyes on me before, but he wears the same insignia I do. And unfailingly he has welcomed me and helped me in my need. Perhaps you have known similar experiences in which the chance sighting of some insignia has changed you, or someone else, from strangers into brothers or sisters.

(3) An insignia sometimes is worn, not to catch the public eye or to win friends and influence people, so much as simply *to serve the wearer as a quiet, personal reminder of the ideals of the group to which one has given allegiance.* Numbers of Christians wear a tiny lapel cross, not to proclaim, "Look how good I am!" but to serve them as a visual reminder of the faith they are called to exemplify. Many more carry a pocket cross which only they and their families know about, so it shall recall to them, privately in the inner chambers of the heart, the Savior who has called them into His service.

And what organization has more treasured insignia than Christianity? There are whole encyclopedias of Christian symbols which have been developed, sometimes through blood, sweat, and tears, to proclaim the faith and the commands it lays on all who believe. There are dozens of crosses, from the simple tau ιο the complex Jerusalem cross; there are fish and Greek-letter combinations which date from the early church; there is the pitcher-and-torch symbol of the modern Gideons and hundreds of others which appeared during the intervening centuries.

But these are not what Paul meant by the insignia of Christ. In his letter to the church folk at Colossae—a group trying to grow into full Christian faith against the pagan influences of a corrupt culture—Paul stated what were the emblems of discipleship these Christians should have worn in order to proclaim their faith and find support from other like-minded persons. In the third chapter he wrote: "Put on the garments that suit God's chosen people, His own, His beloved: compassion, kindness, humility, gentleness, patience. Be forbearing with one another, and forgiving, where any of you has cause for complaint: you must forgive as the Lord forgave you. To crown all, there must be love, to bind all together and complete the whole" (vv. 12-14, NEB). Qualities such as these constitute the basic insignia which you and I must display. To exemplify these qualities habitually will make us stand out in a crowd. "Wear outward emblems if you like," Paul was advising in effect, "but remember that it is only by such personal qualities that you are actually marked as a follower of the Master." *The Christian insignia must ultimately leave the lapel or necklace and become embroidered on our deeds.* The cross must be found not so much on your person and mine as in our hearts.

In his autobiography, Lyman Abbott tells an incident concerning his grandfather, Squire Abbott. About 1860 an uneducated man who had been preaching in schoolhouses and country churches presented himself before a Church Council requesting ordination. During the examination the candidate was asked, "What is your conception of God?"

The man hesitated a moment and then replied, "I conceive that He is some such person as Squire Abbott." It was an unorthodox answer and doubtless did not hasten the man's ordination. *Yet it revealed that Squire Abbott wore the insignia of Christ.*

Christian missionaries in Turkey may not propagandize for their faith. Mission schools are permitted to operate but are closely watched to see that they do not try to convert their students. Why, then, should mission money be spent in maintaining schools there? Here is Mrs. Harry Meyerling's reply: "While Christianity cannot be taught here, it can be caught. Turkish young people can learn a great deal about Christianity by what they see in the habits and actions of our missionaries right while they are being taught English, mathematics, and history. And the government would be surprised to learn the extent to which Christianity *is* being caught!" That is, our representatives in that far-distant land bear the true insignia of Christ so plainly that their faith becomes known without ever a sermon being preached or verbal witness offered.

Thus when you and I learn how to put on compassion and kindliness, meekness and patience, and forgive one another, we will not need to wear any outward emblem of our faith. The insignia of Christ will appear on us without our knowledge, making known to everyone the fact that we have become good and faithful servants of the Master.

> Of symbols there are many kinds and shapes;
>   Tall crosses, hewn from timber, cast in brass;
> Devoutly appliqued on velvet drapes,
>   Or leaded into delicately stained glass;
> The Greek contraction of our Master's name:

The "Chi Rho" and the "I.H.S." combined;
The Holy Spirit's darting tongues of flame;
The Alpha and Omega intertwined.
But these are mere contrivances of art
Unless they be devices which conduct
The Holy Spirit to my inmost heart—
Unless they serve as God's own aqueduct
Down which the living waters roll
To flood the arid reaches of my soul.

—Kendrick Strong

The fruit of the Spirit is love, joy, peace, patience, kindness, goodness, faithfulness, gentleness, self-control; against such there is no law (Gal. 5:22-23).

11.

Leave Elbowroom for the Holy Spirit

Be filled with the Spirit . . . singing and making melody to the Lord with all your heart, always and for everything giving thanks in the name of our Lord Jesus Christ to God the Father (Eph. 5:18-20).

The Acts of the Apostles relates that Peter and others were hailed before the Sanhedrin for continuing to hold evangelistic meetings after being refused a permit. Peter said, "We must obey God rather than men." This defiance enraged many of the Council, and they howled for the prisoners' blood. But a Pharisee named Gamaliel, held in honor by all, stood up and ordered the prisoners removed. Then he said to his fellows, "Be careful lest in self-righteousness you come to think that anyone who believes differently from you about God must be silenced. *Beware lest you believe that everyone's religious experiences must conform to your own to be true.* Don't be too confident that God has committed into your hands alone the ushering in of His kingdom!" (Author's paraphrase).

Gamaliel was mightily concerned lest the Sanhedrin should establish an autocratic tradition of authority which eventually would repudiate any new revelation from God. He was warning them to leave operating space for the power of God to act directly in human affairs.

What this thoughtful man said, therefore, is important for us to remember today. There is an unimaginable amount of spiritual power at work in our world independently of humankind—a Divine Authority operating from beyond human boundaries. Perhaps on rare occasions you and I have been conscious of mighty influences at work which cannot be traced to a human source. During World War II a naval strategist labeled this influence the "Jesus Factor." Christians, however, speak of this direct action of God or the impact of Jesus on today's world by the familiar person of the Godhead, the Holy Spirit.

There are three different attitudes which you and I can assume toward the Holy Spirit.

(1) We can ignore Him, refuse to have any dealings with Him, or deny His reality. This course was followed by some members of the Sanhedrin. But in cutting themselves off from God, they began to wither spiritually without realizing it.

(2) Again, you and I can be contented with whatever insights the Holy Spirit has granted us thus far, shut off the faucet, and become rigid administrators of that truth. Other members of the Sanhedrin had done this. It is a tempting decision because at best we cannot receive very large amounts of divine revelation. Our souls are too small. We are like toasters which operate only on 110 volts and cannot handle fifty thousand volts. Thus only a fraction of what the Holy Spirit offers can pass into our lives, making our little souls glow like twenty-five-watt bulbs.

To recognize how low our wattage really is can be a saving grace, for then we will seek for higher wattage, and in seeking, find. But how often individuals become so enamored of their modest amount of light that they come to regard it as a whole battery of night-baseball floodlights which outshine all other persons' lamps! How tempting it is to think, *Oh boy! God has given me His whole revelation!* And drawing the shades of our souls to shut out any contradictory truth, we begin to insist that other persons unplug their feeble lights and bask in our light. This is what Gamaliel was afraid was happening, and it is something against which you and I must guard.

For as we learn to make elbowroom for the Holy Spirit, the temptation may assail us to believe that we are under compulsion to correct everyone whose experience does not coincide with ours. In *Leave Yourself Alone*, Eugenia Price reveals how she once yielded to that temptation. "As a new Christian," she wrote, "I did what almost every convinced new believer does: I argued with and pressured and antagonized those who did not yet see God in Christ. In Christ I had found forgiveness, so for about fifteen years I banged people over the head with that magnificent truth, using it to 'prove' that I was right and they were wrong."

But gradually the Holy Spirit revealed to her, as she put it, that "God needs no defense from anyone," and that "the slightest hint of self-righteousness is sin." Just as you and I are to leave elbowroom for God to work in your life and mine, so also we are to leave elbowroom for Him to work in the lives of those with whom we disagree. "There often comes a time," she added, "when our part is to shut up and begin to pray!" For as Paul wrote sternly to the Roman Christians, "You then who teach others, will you not teach yourself?" (Rom. 2:21). He was asking if they were so puffed up with their beliefs that there was no room for fresh truth from God. "Do not be haughty, but go about with humble folk. Do not keep thinking how wise you are" (12:16, NEB). Price pinpointed the reason underlying this admonition: "In order for us to receive the peace Jesus felt, He and He alone must stand central. Not our precious opinions, but Christ's." For it is God in Christ, not us, who reconciles people to Himself.

(3) So there is yet another way in which you and I may relate to the Holy Spirit. It is threefold in nature:

(*a*) *by being grateful* for whatever twenty-five-watt knowledge of truth is now ours;

(*b*) *by acting* in the light of that revelation; and

(*c*) *by being receptive to His new truths* which most certainly will
appear when we are prepared to accept them.

This is giving elbowroom for the Holy Spirit.

This means accepting a principle in Japanese art which, if
artists observe it, will cause them to leave some part of their
masterpieces unfinished. Then the viewers, detecting the
incompleteness, can in their "minds' eye" supply what is
missing, thus sharing in the final creation. Now, you and I
are to amplify this principle in our human-divine relationship so that, as we direct our lives through each day's existence, we leave ourselves open for God to do the final
shaping of our personality and the ultimate molding of our
character.

This is a treasured principle of our historic faith: expecting
God to do new and wonderful things for His children. James
K. Feibleman once wrote: "I had a terrible nightmare. I
dreamed that all truths were known." We may literally
thank God that this is not so, and that we may still attune
ourselves to fresh insights. In 1620 John Robinson, minister
of the English Separatist Church in Leyden, preached a fare-
well sermon to those members who were sailing on the
Mayflower to America. Edward Winslow wrote down the substance of what he said, including this: "If God should reveal
anything to us by any other instrument of His, to be as ready
to receive it as ever we were to receive any truth by his
ministry; for He was very confident that the Lord had more
light and truth yet to break forth out of His holy Word."
Here was holy expectation of God's earlier promise: "I will
pour my Spirit upon your descendants,/and my blessing on
your offspring" (Isa. 44:3).

When growing up, I outgrew clothes faster than I outwore them. Consequently, it was I, oftener than not, who received the new clothes and my younger brothers the outgrown ones. Whenever the salesman at George Brothers' Emporium would hold up some article of clothing against me and say, "That is good, rugged quality, Mrs. Strong," my mother would dubiously reply, "But is there room for growth?"

Here is a good question to ask about our spiritual lives!

Then the Spirit of the Lord will come mightily upon you, and you shall prophecy . . . and be turned into another man (1 Sam. 10:6).

12.

Believe in the Power to Become

To all who received him, who believed in his name, he gave power to become children of God (John 1:12).

How well I remember the frantic speed with which British Customs officials in Harwich once processed my baggage so I might catch the noon ferry to the Hook of Holland. But when I arrived breathlessly at the pier, it was to find six feet of water between me and the departing boat. For the first time I learned the poignant meaning of the phrase which hitherto I had used carelessly: "Missing the boat!" A most unreasoning sense of futility swept over me, not so much because Harwich is such a dreadful place to be stranded in (which it is) as because I had been left behind—always a disheartening experience. Life would flow on without me till the midnight boat, and there was nothing to be done about it.

There are times when both you and I have known this sort of frustration because we have felt for a time that life was leaving us behind. It is extremely unsettling—whether for an hour or a year—to feel utterly at the mercy of events too big for us to handle. Once at a World's Fair I entrusted myself to a free-flying toboggan ride which spiraled at terrific speed down a huge, open-topped chute, during which I have never felt more helpless or totally out of control of my own destiny. Now, in like manner, there are occasions when you and I feel that society itself is gripped by mighty forces beyond our meager power to control. Perhaps we have known times when we feel like bits of driftwood dashed about by angry waves, finally to end stranded on a mud flat in some side channel.

But such experiences do not justify discouragement, for resources are available to you and me. Christianity has maintained its witness and vigor because it shows people how to lay hold of those powers. Whether we are beset with social problems or personal ones, there are ways by which we can conquer any sense either of being victimized by life or of being incompetent to handle life victoriously. For John opened his Gospel with Jesus' promise that "to those who recognized his divine nature and welcomed him in faith, he gave the power to become God's own sons" (John 1:12, VV). When you and I are certain that God is not just in His heaven but stands squarely with us during each day's happenings, then no longer need we be as drifting logs tossed by the currents. Rather, our confidence in God's sustaining presence will be to us like a 135-horsepower inboard motor which enables us to move wherever we want to in spite of contrary wind and wave. When we accept the fact that the universe teams up with goodness, we will find ourselves midstream in a current which will bear us toward our goals. The eddies and backwashes are reserved for those who, in Leslie Weatherhead's words, "try to tap the resources of the universe to make a hell for other people." It is they who run aground or are piled up in catastrope. The main channel belongs to you and me when we accept Jesus' testimony about God as true.

When the Old Testament prophet Elisha was in danger of being captured by the Syrian army at Dothan, the servant peered out the window and saw the enemy moving in relentlessly from all sides. In terror the servant cried out,

"Alas, my Master! What shall we do?" There seemed to be no possible escape.

But Elisha answered calmly, "Do not be afraid, for those who are on our side are more than those on theirs." And the Lord opened the servant's eyes, so he saw the surrounding hills covered with horses and chariots of fire (2 Kings 6:16-17, NEB). In that moment of insight, the servant learned that their resources were greater than their problems—which is always heartening to know. This is why one person and God can constitute a majority, and have been doing so before and since the time of Elisha.

The mighty forces unleashed by the Industrial Revolution produced the vast horror of slums in the major cities of Britain. So massive and so dreadful did those blighted areas become that the average Briton felt that here was an evil far too big to overcome. Yet one man, through his steady stream of novels which dramatized and challenged the brutalization of life, set in motion forces which fought and still fight the blight.

Charles Dickens was armed with power from on high, for he believed that slum people had the right to live as God's children. And similarly, it was the entrance of one man, Emile Zola, into the celebrated affair of French military injustice, the Dreyfus case, with his courageous book *I Accuse!* and his continued attack, which turned the tide in favor of the innocent captain. Neither Dickens nor Zola regarded themselves as helpless souls cast up on some mud bank. Both felt they were part of an unseen majority.

Years ago my brother Robert held the post of chargè d'affaires in the absence of an ambassador at the United States Embassy in Nationalist China. Once a number of our merchant ships were shelled in the Yangtze River by units of the Nationalist navy. When he presented our government's stiff protest, a Chinese admiral replied, "But I told our warships to shoot only at their rudders."

My brother replied coldly, "Whether you were shooting at their rudders or their engine rooms, you were still shooting at American ships. And the United States government will tolerate no ships flying the American flag to be made rudderless and put adrift in the Yangtze River!"

Nor does God want this to happen to you and me. Indeed, no person who flies the Christian flag ever need be rudderless and adrift, at the mercy of treacherous currents he or she cannot control. Resources sufficient for every need are available from God. I have long known that God does not permit any duty or burden to weigh me down unless He gives me the strength to handle it. Paul understood this truth when he wrote to the Corinthian Christians, "He who supplies seed to the sower and bread for food will supply and multiply your resources and increase the harvest of your righteousness" (2 Cor. 9:10).

Thus whenever a sense of helplessness in the face of trouble sweeps over me, I can conquer any incipient panic by thinking, *This problem is a tough one indeed. It demands more ability than I possess. But I know where I can get more. For I have within me the Power to Become!*

Just how does this transfusion of divine power into your feebleness and mine take place? Well, we discover it by sharing the common life of those who are seeking the same resources, that is, by sharing a church fellowship's growing life through worship and service projects, study groups, and outreach efforts. But again, we also grow in spiritual maturity through our own private quests, through Bible reading, through the daily discipline of inward prayer and familiarity with great devotional literature, as well as through a deepening awareness of personal revelation which God at times is pleased to make known directly to our souls. And we also lay hold of spiritual resources when we deepen our personal relation to Jesus, through Whom the power of God continually flows.

To believe in the "power to become," to build our lives on its promise, is to replace disillusionment with vision, pessimism with confidence, and futility with faith.

[May you] be filled with the knowledge of his will in all spiritual wisdom and understanding, to lead a life worthy of the Lord, fully pleasing to him, bearing fruit in every good work and increasing in the knowledge of God. May you be strengthened with all power, according to his glorious might, for all endurance and patience with joy (Col. 1:9-11).

13.

Start Living Today as Though Immortal

The world passes away, and the lust of it; but he who does the will of God abides forever (1 John 2:17).

If you enjoy camping but are bothered by the intense heat which can build up within your tent, you have no doubt discovered a practical solution. You can buy a large tarpaulin and stretch it across a second ridgepole twelve inches higher than the tent. Such a fly sheet receives the direct punishment from the sun while circulation in the airspace underneath keeps the tent itself from becoming stifling. You are setting a new, larger tent over the original one.

This is an ancient practice which originated in those lands where the climate is fiercely hot and where tents provide most of the housing. So brisk was the demand for tents in Paul's day that he plied his trade of tentmaking throughout the Roman Empire. Some of Paul's skill must have gone into making such fly sheets, for he uses the idea as a metaphor to explain eternal life. In his second letter to the Corinthian church, Paul wrote:

> We know that if the earthly frame that houses us today should be demolished, we possess a building which God has provided—a be demolished, we possess a building which God has provided—a house not made by human hands, eternal, and in heaven. In this present body we do indeed groan;

we yearn to have our heavenly habitation put on over this one—in the hope that, being thus clothed, we shall not find ourselves naked. We groan indeed, we who are enclosed within this earthly frame; we are oppressed because we do not want to have the old body stripped off. Rather, our desire is to have the new body put on over it, so that our mortal part may be absorbed into life immortal. God himself has shaped us for this very end; and as a pledge of it he has given us the Spirit (2 Cor. 5:1-4, NEB).

Immortality, then, is not just something which we may come into when we die, if we have loved the Lord. Rather, it is God's free gift, *which we are able to fit on over our present life like an extra coat. Above our mortal tents you and I may stretch the tent of eternity!*

This belief is not peculiar to Paul, for John had made a similar discovery: "Truly, I say to you, he who hears my words and believes him who sent me, has eternal life; he does not come into judgment, but has passed from death into life" (John 5:24). Already such believers partake of immortality, right now, here in this life!

What a hope this offers you and me! For which of life's problems and troubles are not answered by this assurance? When we accept that Jesus can be our Savior, we have a means of conquering our entrenched habit of doing sinful, stupid, or thoughtless things.

Now, I acknowledge that it is not the "in thing" these days to talk about sin. The new psychology declares that the whole concept of sin "is tied to antiquated Jehovistic morality." Yet you and I most certainly do sin—not terribly perhaps but continuously, in the New Testament sense. For the Greek word used for "sin" is *hamartia,* an archery term which simply means "missing the mark"—not hitting what you should be shooting at. This metaphor makes sense to me because the two times I have held a bow in my hands, I have not only failed to hit the target but the entire butt, and most of my time was spent in retrieving arrows from the woods.

To me, therefore, sin indeed is "missing the mark." Through my knowledge of the Bible, through the example of friends and my own experience, and through my efforts to discover the mind of Christ, I know almost exactly what God wants me to be shooting at in each day's living. I am well aware that temptation, laziness, or indifference at times cause me to pull off the target and miss the mark. *Sin is going in* this *self-calculating direction when God is urging me in* that *totally different direction.* All too often my "arrows" hit my target and not God's. What can be done about it?

Over the tent of our earthly sins and failures you and I may stretch the canvas of Divine forgiveness. This is God's promise through the lips of Jesus. This tent of eternity is ours for the taking.

Such confidence can remove the sting from any dread of the future. Although you and I do not think about it much, over everyone hangs the deadly possibility of accidental or intentional nuclear war. Some individuals are worried about the fast-approaching day when they can no longer earn their own living but must spend the remainder of their days within the rigid framework of their retirement income. Over others hangs the threat of unemployment, major surgery, or extended illness, which can wipe out both health and life savings in one cruel blow. And with accidents and criminal violence at all-time highs, chief among many individuals is the fear of sudden death.

Crises like these offer real threats to your life and mine. They are genuine dangers, and we cannot deny their reality, but we must face them boldly. Through the example of Jesus, God is continually reminding us that whatever our sins and failures, whatever our loneliness, our dread of the future or fear of death, these no longer need have dominion over us. This is possible because we have the assurance that over our everyday living may be stretched the tarpaulin of God's nearer presence, the tent of eternity.

Today you and I may start living as though we are immortal—and in Christ we are.

> You also must consider yourselves dead to sin and alive to God in Christ Jesus. Let not sin therefore reign in your mortal bodies, to make you obey their passions. Do not yield your members to sin as instruments of wickedness, but yield yourselves to God as men who have been brought from death to life (Rom. 6:11-13).

14.

Cherish a Vision of Your Promised Land

And in the Spirit [the angel] carried me away to a great, high mountain, and showed me the holy city Jerusalem coming down out of heaven from God, having the glory of God, its radiance like a most rare jewel, like jaspar, clear as crystal (Rev. 21:10-11).

Once as we drove eastward from the Olympic Peninsula toward Mount Rainier in pouring rain, my wife and I traveled through forests worked by huge lumber companies. Shortly we saw a sign which read, "PROMISED LAND, 30 MILES." This intrigued us, for at regular intervals there followed other signs reading twenty miles, then fifteen, ten, five, miles, and finally, a thousand yards. Soon we would discover how the State of Washington interpreted an Old Testament term.

Then came the big sign, "WELCOME TO THE PROMISED LAND! PROVIDED FOR YOU BY THE RAYONIER LUMBER COMPANY." This was something of a letdown because the original one had been provided by the Lord God Almighty. But there, across a little rushing stream, set in a beautiful grove of Douglas fir, was an attractive campground bustling with people. Just as we slowed down to look, the sun poked through the clouds and set the raindrops to sparkling on tents and tables, fireplaces, and tree branches. It was, indeed, the kind of promised land which all tourists pulling trailers or campers like to dream about awaiting them at the end of a long afternoon. We know from our own camping experience that the day passes more happily when such anticipation and expectancy spices each hour. Directories of camp sites have psychological as well as practical uses!

But one of the earliest of family campers, the patriarch Abraham, had neither directories nor prepared campsites available to him. "By faith," states Hebrews, "Abraham obeyed when he was called to go out to a place which he was to receive as an inheritance; and he went out, not knowing where he was to go. By faith he sojourned in the land of promise, as in a foreign land" (Heb. 11:8). Abraham had no map, but he accepted God's word that there was indeed a Promised Land for him and his descendants.

This promise of a land flowing with milk and honey profoundly influenced the escaping Hebrew slaves under Moses' leadership. God indeed had provided a haven within which they could end their nomadic wanderings and put down the roots needed to produce a great nation. And if you have followed the course of Zionism for the past sixty years, you know something of what the cry "the Promised Land" —now the State of Israel—has meant to endangered Judaism the world over.

Of course, the whole westward thrust of our American empire was inspired by this same kind of dream. Columbus, Ponce de Leon, Sir Walter Raleigh, and Samuel de Champlain, all of whom explored and attempted to colonize our eastern coast, were spurred by a vision of heaven on earth. Prompted by such a dream, James Oglethorpe secured the release of many individuals from debtors' prisons and led them to America to found the colony of Georgia. It was related by F. Van Wyck Mason that as the heavily-laden ship came into Charleston Harbor,

> a big, beetle-browed fellow jumped up on to the bow-sprint and, clinging to a stay, yelled back to the quarterdeck, "God

bless ye, Governor, ye've brought us out o' jail and fetched us safe and sound to the Promised Land!" And a great shout of joy and of commendation to the leader arose from the ship.[3]

And there was Marcus Whitman, a missionary doctor, who sought a Promised Land on the far Northwest frontier; after great hardships he founded a settlement at Walla Walla. Insistently, Whitman petitioned Congress to annex the Pacific Northwest before Great Britain snatched it. His most powerful opponent was "Divine Dan'l" Webster, who had just bought land in Wisconsin for speculation and felt that this was far enough West for any good American to venture. Speaking about the Oregon country one day in the Senate chamber, Webster exclaimed, "What do we want with this vast, worthless area, this land of savages and wild beasts, of shifting sands and whirlwinds of dust? To what use could we ever put those endless mountain ranges, impenetrable and covered to their base with eternal snows? Mr. President, I will never vote one cent from the public treasury to put the Pacific coast one inch nearer to Boston than it is now!"

To counter such blathering, Whitman made the perilous journey back to Washington to argue his case in person. Fortunately, influential people listened to him rather than to the golden-tongued orator. For it was Whitman, in searching for his Promised Land, promoting it passionately, and ultimately paying for it with his life—and not the renowned Daniel Webster—who was finally responsible for bringing the states of Washington and Oregon into the Union.

There are many kinds of promised lands, and they are not all geographical. Indeed, behind every thought of a physical location has been a spiritual dream, the geographic area being simply a realization of that dream in the here and now. Both you and I have known such inward visions, wherein we hunger for some condition of life—whether material or spiritual—which is significantly better than what we are now experiencing. And the influence of such secret commitments often holds us steady over the rough stretches of our daily living. "We walk by faith, not by sight" (2 Cor. 5:7).

Common to the instances mentioned above was the conviction that God Himself had made ready a promised land and was leading His people there. *This meant that each venture was embued with a sense of holiness.* The pilgrims' hopes were grounded and sustained in a sense of the sacred. Thus if you and I are to accept this guideline, there must be a holy dimension to whatever Promised Land we seek. For only then will we become, in the quest, the richly-rounded persons whom God envisioned when He made us.

This means that whatever Promised Land we cherish must dovetail into the vision of the Kingdom which God has planned for us. We are indeed to look for "new heavens and a new earth in which righteousness dwells" (2 Pet. 3:13). Then as we move toward realizing those dreams, you and I will also grow into citizenship within that Kingdom.

I am persuaded that no authentic promised land is too far away for you and me to reach. All that is required of us is that we shall be faithful.

> In him you also, who have heard the word of truth, the gospel of your salvation, and have believed in him, were sealed with the promised Holy Spirit, which is the guarantee of our inheritance until we acquire possession of it, to the praise of his glory (Eph. 1:13-14).

15.

Discover that Love is Stronger than Fear

God did not give us a spirit of timidity but a spirit of power and love and self-control (2 Tim. 1:6-7).

The daughter of a famous British actor once wrote:

> My father was infected with hypochondria. He never moved without a perfect battery of pills and medicines. Absolutely certain that he had heart trouble, he once consulted a heart specialist who gave him thorough tests. Finally the specialist said gravely, "Mr. _____, I'm afraid you have an incurable disease."
>
> "Yes, yes!" said Father, "I knew it, I knew it! Tell me, what is it?"
>
> "Fear!" came the brief reply.

How tragic! You and I, of course, live in a fear-ridden world. Anxiety and concern could easily be let loose in our lives to gnaw like little mice if we would permit ourselves to be infected by the fearfulness of those around us. Yet we, of all people, ought most easily to be victorious over our fears which threaten our peace of mind and our creative output.

Among the church's youth there is a demand that she become actively involved in social change, whereas among adults there is also present a contrary insistence that the church shall include a fear-deadening sense of comfort. But both are right. For as Bishop Charles Gore has pointed out,

"The Christian religion is a religion of comfort. *Confortare* [Latin], with its Greek original, means first of all, 'to make strong' or 'to encourage.' Religion is to put heart and courage into us." When Isaiah wrote, "Comfort ye, comfort ye my people, saith your God," the Lord was saying through him, Become strong, become fearless, My people! *This is what Christianity is about.*

When Dorothy Alexander moved from Kansas to Florida she sent a sample of her proposed garden soil to the Department of Agriculture for analysis. She received this answer: "The Department is sad to report that our analysis of your soil indicates that it needs everything except sand." Now this may have been bad for her garden, but it can serve well as a parable. For if in her own character she had an equivalent amount of "sand," she could keep at bay any evil shapes of fearfulness which can maim or destroy personality. "Sand" is one of the essential ingredients of Christlike character.

How, then, do you and I acquire the necessary "sand" to conquer fear? How do we deal with the apprehensions and anxieties which sometimes slip through our defenses? The power to cast out evil spirits was resident in Jesus, and it can also be resident in us. The source of that power was revealed when John wrote, "God is love, and he who abides in love abides in God, and God abides in him. . . . There is no fear in love, but perfect love casts out fear" (1 John 4:16-17).

A veteran World War I news correspondent visited America after the Armistice. Highly honored and popular though he was, Philip Gibbs was a shy, unassuming man. And when he was gently pushed out onto the stage at Carnegie Hall where he faced a huge audience, this man who had faced artillery fire in the trenches suddenly was paralyzed by stage fright. His mouth went dry, his hands trembled, his knees weakened. But as he tried to get enough saliva together to start his opening sentence, he was struck by a fresh fear. He wrote: "There was a sudden movement like a tidal wave among all those people. It was as though they were advancing on me, possibly with intent to kill!"

But then it swept over him that they were paying him a great honor. They all had spontaneously risen to their feet to show that they loved him. As Sir Philip became conscious of their affection reaching out to envelop him, his stage fright died away, his trembling ceased, his saliva began to flow, and he was able to proceed with his lecture. Of that event, he reported, "It was that spirit of friendship and good-will reaching out to me that gave me courage." Exactly!

Now, just how do you and I get this "perfect love" to work on our behalf? There is an excellent summary of its ingredients in the "love chapter" of Paul's letter to the Christian colony in Corinth. In the thirteenth chapter the apostle passed the pure light of perfect love through the prism of daily experiences, breaking it up into its component colors. In this early Christian hymn Paul listed the practical daily virtues which we are to acquire, the sum total of which become love. As we become skilled in their use we gain the capacity to be victors over fear.

Here is the heart of Paul's list:

> Love is patient and kind; love is not jealous or boastful; it is
> not arrogant or rude. Love does not insist on its own way;
> it is not irritable or resentful; it does not rejoice at wrong, but
> rejoices in the right. Love bears all things, believes all things,
> hopes all things, endures all things. Love never ends (1 Cor.
> 13:4-8).

When you and I succeed in fusing such qualities as these with our daily experiences, we will have the perfect love which casts out fear.

In her moving book about her missionary parents entitled *The Exile,* Pearl Buck related how her mother, Carie, at great personal danger, had saved their housekeeper, Wang Amah, from painful death from cholera. Later Wang Amah asked her wonderingly, "What woman are you, and what a heart is this, that for a common brown creature like me whom none other has ever cared to see twice, you would give your life?"

"Carie was abashed by such worship," her daughter added, "and later she confided that if she had stopped to think about the danger of contracting cholera herself, she would never have done it." But so great was her affection and concern for Wang Amah that she had waded in and vanquished the killer disease without considering possible personal consequences. The love of Christ controlled her (2 Cor. 5:14).

The acquiring of such self-forgetting love, of course, requires determination. Only practice makes perfect. But as we purposefully begin to use the list of ingredients listed by Paul, here a little, there a little, moving toward an enlarging kindliness and gentleness, humility and courtesy, selflessness and holiness in everyday situations, *we will find ourselves no longer victims of life but victors over life!* Then we shall especially appreciate Longfellow's lines:

> And the night shall be filled with music,
> And the cares that infest the day,
> Shall fold their tents, like the Arabs,
> And as silently steal away.

For as we discover that love is stronger than fear, we will grow into the mind of Christ.

Love is strong as death; . . . Many waters cannot quench love, neither can the floods drown it (Song 8:6-7, KJV).

16.

Maintain a Forward Momentum

One thing I do, forgetting what lies behind and straining forward to what lies ahead, I press on toward the goal for the prize of the upward call in Christ Jesus (Phil. 3:13-14).

The picturesque metaphor, "Between the devil and the deep, blue sea," describes a predicament from which there appears to be no escape. Apparently the one who coined it neither knew how to swim nor how to deal with the devil, which is the subject of a later guideline: there are remedies for both situations! But because this metaphor speaks only of two possible choices, neither of which is any good, I doubt that it accurately describes most of the predicaments which beset you and me. This is so because usually there are further choices, not at first apparent, which can offer useful or creative solutions to the difficulty. For religious faith and holy imagination may offer timely rescue!

There was a day when a particular people felt that they were indeed caught between the devil and the sea, and they were the children of Israel when fleeing northeastwardly from slavery. The devil was the Egyptian Pharaoh leading the pursuit in his golden chariot, thundering ever nearer in a rolling cloud of dust. And the "deep, blue sea" was the Red Sea which lay across the Israelites' path as solidly as though it were the Great Wall of China. Along the marshy edges they would be helplessly pinned by the furious Egyptians.

The biblical record continues: "Pharaoh was almost upon

them when the Israelites looked up and saw the Egyptians close behind. In their terror they clamoured to the Lord for help and said to Moses, 'Were there no graves in Egypt, that you should have brought us here to die in the wilderness?' " (NEB).

Moses sought to reassure them. "Have no fear, . . . stand firm and see the deliverance that the Lord will bring you this day; for as sure as you see the Egyptians now, you will never see them again." But they shouted him down.

So Moses went off to consult with God, who promptly spoke to him two of the great sentences of the Bible: "What is the meaning of this clamor? Tell the Israelites to strike camp." Then He added, "And you shall raise high your staff, stretch out your hand over the sea and cleave it in two, so that the Israelites can pass through the sea on dry ground" (Ex. 14:10-16, NEB).

"Wherefore criest thou unto me?" reads the King James Version. "Speak to the children of Israel, that they go forward" (v. 15).

So while fog pinned down the enemy, Moses went down to the shore and stretched his staff over the water. A strong East wind began to blow, which continued all night, powerful enough to push the waters westward till the shallow bottom lay bare. By sunup there was a way of escape, and the Israelites crossed the barrier dry-shod. Everyone knows what happened to the pursuing Egyptians when Moses stretched forth his staff again, and the waters rolled back into place (see vv. 21-28).

"When Israel saw the great power which the Lord had put forth against Egypt, all the people feared the Lord, and they put their faith in him" (v. 31, NEB).

"Tell the Israelites to strike camp." There was no other sensible choice for them, nor for you and me today. *Life does not permit our giving up and turning back—not if we are to live victori-*

ously. Remembrance of the past, of course, is a vital and precious part of our existence. To understand the present and guide it properly into the future, we must have a thoughtful awareness of past experiences and what they have taught us. Yet nostalgia—intensified hunger for the "good old days"—simply for itself alone is a treacherous emotion. For example, it can warp my present-day judgments by giving past experiences greater value than they possessed; it entices me to look backward more enthusiastically than forward; it prevents hope from becoming dominant within me because it persuades me that today's opportunities are only second-rate; and it kills the vibrant heart of faith within me, drowning God's present and future promises of more rewarding living. Nostalgia can petrify a Christian so gradually that one becomes a mere religious fossil!

The theologian Gabriel Fackre has introduced a helpful new word *aiglatson,* meaning readiness to move toward the not-yet. Although it has a Greek sound, it is simply *nostalgia* spelled backward. God is where the forward action is, providing as of old the "pillar of cloud by day and the column of fire by night," opening paths ahead where no path at all can be seen. You and I possess "aiglatson" when we fully commit ourselves, continually to be striking camp and following the leading of the Lord, reaching out confidently toward the not-yet. Teilhard de Chardin observed, "What finally divides the individuals today into two camps is not class, but an attitude of mind—the spirit of forward movement." That is, *the aiglatsonists sense a momentum in history and in contemporary life directed by God.* Wasn't this what Tennyson meant by the whole creation moving toward some far-off, divine event? God has so much He wants to reveal to each of us ahead!

As I grow older, as I have been doing for well over seventy

years, I am tempted to recycle the good experiences of yes-
teryears into today's living, even though present conditions
and circumstances are radically different now. I have needed
at times to be reminded that God is not just the God of
Abraham, Isaac, and Jacob, but He is also the God of my
wife and myself, and of my children and grandchildren
down to the nth generation; and I am to move forward with
Him in utmost confidence.

Marcus Whitman was mentioned in the fourteenth guideline as a missionary who with his bride established in 1835
a mission to the Northwest Coast Indians. In 1842 he made
the hard journey back East to plead for more settlers to the
Oregon country and more money for his mission. He sought
out Daniel Webster for assistance, but the senator dismissed
Whitman's please, saying abruptly, "There cannot be made
a wagon road over the mountains. Sir George Simpson says
so."

Sir George had traveled West as far as Colorado where
there are twenty-eight peaks over twelve thousand feet
high. He took one look and exclaimed, "All roads end here!"
and fled back to the coziness of New England. But whenever
Whitman encountered a barrier on his way West, he kept
forging ahead, searching out hidden mountain passes, creating what became the famous Oregon Trail. So Whitman's
reply to Webster is an American classic, simply, *"There is a
road, for I have made it!"*

So, as you and I yield to the forward momentum which
is built into all creative living, we will grow into greater
self-realization.

> This command [God] gave them: "Obey my voice, and I will
> be your God, and you shall be my people; and walk in all the
> way that I command you, that it may be well with you" (Jer.
> 7:23).

17.

Always Face Eastward

They shall reverence the name of the Lord in the sunset, and his glory in the sunrise (Isa. 59:19, VV).

So we are to maintain momentum. In what direction?

A young man just home from the American Civil War accosted Horace Greeley with this question: "Sir, where do you believe may be found the best openings in America for a man of purpose and ability?"

Without hesitation the publisher gave this now-famous reply: "Go West, young man, go West!" There lay the land of opportunity.

This sentence eventually became our country's major expansion slogan, which fueled our sense of "Manifest Destiny." There followed a remarkable developmental period in our history, illustrating the observation of George Berkeley, bishop of Cloyne, in 1792: "Westward the course of empire takes its way."

Our history indeed has had a Western orientation. The frontiers which beckoned to the ceaseless stream of European immigrants were always toward the sunset. Golden opportunities lay toward the West. Colonel Zane and others opened the "Western Reserve," and Daniel Boone settled the "dark and bloody ground" of Kentucky. Homesteaders filled the prairie states, and wagon trains creaked out from Independence and Council Bluffs. Adventurers pushed into

the Rockies and on to gold-flecked California—one area
giving way to a new one always further West—till suddenly
we ran out of Western frontiers. Now you and I must shift
orientation to other types of frontiers—social, economic,
and spiritual—giving them the same dramatic attention and
dynamic fulfillment which we brought to the westering
frontier. *To do this we must face in a different direction.*

For historical reasons much of our nation's thinking has
been westerly-oriented. And indeed, the life-style of most
Americans today causes most of us to see a hundred sunsets
for every one sunrise. Thus, the sun's rising does not color
our thinking or feeling as does the sun's setting. This is a
shame, for the symbols and metaphors which are derived
from "the dawn's early light" are closer to the Christian
outlook than a sunset ever can be. For consider these
thoughts:

(1) When you face West you eventually head into the
fading day and the night which the sunset heralds. In Shakespeare's *Richard the Third* is this comment: "When the sun
sets, who does not look for night?" Naturally! But Christians
are not to look for night at any time in their lives! Of course,
for me to welcome the end of a particularly wearisome day
can indeed be a wholesome feeling, greeting the sunset with
joy because I can quit work and rest my aching bones. *But
this attitude becomes unwholesome when I turn its metaphor of "quitting
for the day" into a cop-out from dealing aggressively with social and moral
problems.* Is it not "facing West" for you or me to believe that
any time we feel tired—or retired—we can give up the battle
against wrongs and relax into carefree forgetfulness? For the
hymn does not read:

> Sit down, O men of God,
> And say to all, "Good night!

I've earned the right to nod;
Let George those evils fight.

Rather, are we not to sing, "Christian, up and smite them"? For us to close up shop on issues of immense concern to humankind is not how God expects us to behave.

(2) By further extension of the metaphor, "facing West" can also give a negative meaning to death. During World War I there appeared a euphemism to replace the harsh statement of battle casualty. When a doughboy was killed in action, he was spoken of as having "gone West." And this meant literally not the sunset but rather the blackness of the grave. But this is not a Christian attitude toward death. On the tomb of Dr. Edward Increase Bosworth of Oberlin College is a better description. It reads, "INTO THE LIGHT!" Yes, Jesus' followers have a different compass orientation, for they do not think of death either as terminating in darkness or the grave.

What, then, shall your compass orientation and mine be? The answer is perfectly simple: we are to face East! We are to be oriented not to the sunset, however breathtaking, with its inevitable night. Rather, we are to be oriented toward the sunrise and its inevitable day. "From the rising of the sun to its setting, the name of the Lord is to be praised!" (Ps. 113:3). We are to look Eastward, into the light!

The prophetic vision of Ezekiel endorses this. Early in his ministry, Ezekiel witnessed the departure of the Lord from Jerusalem because of that city's wickedness. But when its people repented and sought forgiveness for their sins, there came a time when God returned with healing, redeeming power. Ezekiel described it thus: "He led me to the gate, the gate facing eastwards, and I beheld the glory of the God of Israel coming from the East. His voice was like the sound of a mighty torrent, and the earth shone with his glory" (Ezek. 43:1-2, NEB). Twenty years earlier there had been a sunset followed by blackest night. Now there was sunrise, followed by the splendor of a new day for Israel.

This symbolism has been carried over into the New Testament. Jesus was born in the East, and at His birth there came Wise Men, not from the West from where we think all wisdom now flows, but from the East. And it was "as it began to dawn" that the knowledge of the resurrection burst on the two Marys at the sepulcher. Later, both Peter's Second Epistle and the Book of Revelation describe describe the Holy Spirit as a "star of dawn" Who rises to illumine our hearts. And one of the loveliest metaphors ever applied to Jesus—now unused and all but forgotten—is found in the closing verses of Revelation: "I am the bright and morning star" (v. 16). As Jesus' followers, then, we look not to Tannhauser's "sublime, sweet evening star," but to the "bright star of dawn." This is to be our orientation.

How do I begin a new day? Do I drag myself out of bed, thinking, "Oh my, today has arrived sooner than I wanted it to. I wonder if I can make it through the next sixteen hours?" That is "facing west," which is still dark.

Or do I arise buoyantly, thinking, *"This is the day which the Lord has made; [I will] rejoice and be glad in it"?* (Ps. 118:24). This is facing East!

How do I face changes in social customs and moral attitudes, the increase in drug defilement and white-collar crime, all of which seems to be turning our nation into a disturbing, strange nightmare? Do I moan and groan that humankind has nothing but gloom and doom ahead? That is facing the fading light. Or, *am I expectant that under God our nation is redeemable, so that I live on life's forward edge of hope?* Am I of the same mind as Justice Douglas who said, "There's a fine group of people in this country who badly want to do the right thing. . . . I think the heart of America is sound. I think the conscience of America is bright. I think the future of America is great"? This is facing the glory of the sunrise.

How do I endure sickness or tragedy? Do I settle down under the black mantle of hopelessness, stoically or resentfully waiting for it to pass? That is facing the West, from which no dawn ever comes. *Or do I go, as it were, to an East window and maintain a steady vigil,* as did the psalmist: "Out of the depths have I called to thee, O Lord; My soul waits for the Lord more eagerly than watchmen for the morning" (130:1,6, NEB). This imagery is made more poignant when I remember certain nights of pain when each minute became an hour, the darkness turned pitiless, and fearfulness and despair crept to the foot of my bed. But I can also recall how the first pale signs of dawn stole through the window, bringing a miracle of relief and vitality to my heart. This comes from facing East.

Thus it is essential that in spite of the value of recollection, the bulk of your looking and mine must be toward the East, with confidence and expectancy and with the companionship of "the bright and Morning Star," the ever-rising Christ! Of course there will be evils to subdue, demons to exorcise, and ghosts to lay to rest. *But none of these can survive the sunrise of God's glory as it shines in your face and mine.* Shakespeare knew this. In *Midsummer Night's Dream,* he described the coming dawn:

> For night's swift dragons cut the clouds full fast,
> And yonder shines Aurora's harbinger;
> At whose approach, ghosts, wandering here and there,
> Troop home to churchyards.

And to their tombs! Exactly! Ghosts, demons, and wickedness cannot stand any dawn as it breaks over the eastern hills. You and I grow in spiritual maturity as we are warmed, as was Ezekiel, by the glory of God coming from the East!

The night is far gone, the day is at hand. Let us then cast off the works of darkness and put on the armor of light; let us conduct ourselves becomingly as in the day (Rom. 13:13).

18.
Accept Responsibility for Yourself

As they were at table eating, Jesus said, "Truly, I say to you, one of you will betray me, one who is eating with me." They began to be sorrowful, and to say to him one after another, "Is it I?" (Mark 14:18-19).

Simon found pleasure in poor health, enjoying complaining about his ills. One day when his doctor was lecturing him about an especially complaining mood, Simon exclaimed petulantly, "See here, you can't blame me for my poor physical condition. All my family was that way. I weigh 230 now, but I was very delicate as a child. Why, my mother states that when I was born I weighed only seven pounds!" Simon was able to maintain a comforting fiction of ill health because he refused to acknowledge being a responsible person. "Don't blame me. Blame my physical heritage —the kind of genetic chain I received from my parents. It's all their fault that I am what I am!"

"Don't blame me" is a sentence straight from the Garden of Eden. When God asked Adam if he had eaten the forbidden fruit, Adam replied, "W-e-ll, that woman You gave me, she tempted me." And Eve quickly interjected, "But it was that serpent over there who put me up to it!" And the rascally serpent, who could find no one to blame, nervously shuffled the feet he was so soon to lose.

Then later came Aaron, Moses' brother and the high priest. Exodus deals with events of perhaps thirty-five-hundred years ago, but how often its people behaved pretty much as you and I do! The thirty-second chapter relates that when the Israelites were camped at Mount Sinai, Moses went up the mountain for literally a literal summit meeting with the Almighty. When he failed to return when expected, the people easily talked Aaron into making a golden fertility idol which they might worship after the orgiastic manner of the pagans around them. When Moses returned, he destroyed the golden calf and furiously questioned Aaron, "Why did you do so evil a thing?"

His brother replied uneasily, "Don't be so upset. You know that these people are set on evil. They said to me, 'Make us a god,' and they brought me all their gold. I threw it into the fire, and out came this calf! The miracle wasn't my doing, not at all! It was the people's idea. They're responsible for getting heathen worship going in camp."

"Why blame me?" Aaron sounds positively modern! "I'm not responsible. Go and accuse someone else!" How much we hear this today, and it is bad for our social and moral order. In his delightful book *Earth Could Be Fair*, Pierre van Paassen drew a portrait of his Netherlands hometown of Gorcum from 1907 to 1945. He told about his boyhood friends who grew up alongside him in the warm environment of Christian homes, both Catholic and Protestant, and who, developing into responsible persons, interested themselves in the moral and social problems of the village. They were the ones who became heroic leaders of the Dutch Resistance during the tragic Nazi occupation of Holland. He gave names and specific examples. And conversely, he showed that those boyhood acquaintances who grew up irresponsibly without the guidance either of a Christian home or church became the ones who collaborated with the Nazis, betraying their own countrymen in order to ensure their own safety.

Thus personal irresponsibility lays a heavy weight on society. All around, aren't we conscious of certain religious, moral, social, and educational disintegration? Are we doomed to see such cracks widen endlessly? Not at all, for there are courses of action you and I can take, which can help us produce a stronger sense of personal responsibility both in ourselves and in our communities.

(1) *We can learn to recognize the specious and fraudulent arguments used to perpetuate the "Why-blame-me?" syndrome.* We cannot annihilate an enemy until we identify it. So it will be useful to list several of the excuses used to avoid accepting blame.

(a) One such excuse emerges out of the doctrine of original sin. There is much to be said for this belief, for it offers a logical explanation for demonic human behavior. But this belief can be misused to protect and entrench the very demonic power it describes. *It implies that irresponsibility and unaccountability are inseparable parts of our natural makeup.* We have been like that since the Garden of Eden. "In Adam's fall we sinned all." The cop-out becomes: we are innocent victims of our own inherent weaknesses and cannot be held responsible for anything we do. Spurious argument number one.

(b) Another enemy to unmask is pseudosociological in nature. We hear the claim that *human beings are so much at the mercy of environmental forces beyond their control that the only ones truly blameable for individuals' shortcomings are those who control the power structures of community and nation.* There is a certain truth to this claim, but not when people use it as an alibi by saying, "You can't blame me. Blame the Capitalist system, blame war, blame Communism, or the broken home or slum in which I grew up." Spurious argument number two.

(c) Perhaps you were exposed to a third enemy in your college psychology course. It is the argument of determinism —that *we are helpless victims of tensions, pressures, and circumstances too great for our psyches to control.* You and I are bundles of suppressed desires, fierce unrecognized hungers, and per-

sonality distortions. We are shaped inexorably by com-
plexes and phobias. Spurious argument number three.

(d) And these enemies are overshadowed by a modern
school of theology which stresses God's complete powerful-
ness and our own utter helplessness. We can do nothing at
all to save ourselves. *Only God is able to make improvements in you
and me: if He doesn't, how can we be blamed?* In His own good time
and in His own mysterious way, He will bring us into whatever salvation He has purposed for us. Of course, there is
truth in this belief, yet no one may use it properly as a reason
for failing to be a responsible disciple of Jesus. Here is the
most dangerous argument, spurious argument number four.
Indeed, all these assumptions are pure hokum, cunning and
enticing excuses prepared by clever people *to rid themselves of
the guilt of doing bad things and of not doing Christlike things.*

(2) A second suggestion about what we can do, is *to keep
stricter tabs on our own excuse making.* We will resolve to stop
passing any buck or dodging any responsibility or assigning
blame to everyone but ourselves. Thomas Nast's most famous cartoon of the 1880s depicted Boss Tweed and his
Tammany Hall cronies under the caption: "Who stole the
people's money?" The group is standing in a closed circle
facing out, and each member is pointing a thumb at the
person on his right. "Don't blame *me! He* did it!" The power
of the cartoon is found in its intimation that the proper
answer of each individual should have been to point the
thumb toward himself: "I did it! I'm to blame!"

At a meeting of the International Sunday School Associa-
tion in England, there hung a huge banner bearing the
words: "Lord, Revive Thy Church—Beginning with Me."
Here are our marching orders. When Jesus predicted to the
disciples at the Last Supper, "One of you will betray Me,"
they did not exclaim, "Well, Lord, is it that fellow over

there?" No indeed. They had been with Jesus too long for that kind of response.

Instead, deeply troubled, each one asked, "Lord, is it I?"

In similar fashion you and I may grow in spiritual discernment as we learn to accept full responsibility for ourselves.

> Judah said to Israel [Jacob], "Send the lad [Benjamin] with me, . . . I will be surety for him; of my hand you shall require him. If I do not bring him back to you and set him before you, then let me bear the blame forever" (Gen. 43:8-9).

BELMONT COLLEGE LIBRARY

19.
Learn to Handle Life's Interruptions

This slight momentary affliction is preparing for us an eternal weight of glory beyond all comparison (2 Cor. 4:17).

Have you ever dreamed a poem into existence, complete with rhyme and rhythm, so you could write it down? Samuel Taylor Coleridge, the nineteenth-century British poet, actually composed an epic poem while asleep. On awaking, Coleridge hastened to his desk in order to write it down while it was vividly in mind. He was just well launched on "Kubla Khan" and had finished transcribing the lines: "For he on honeydew hath fed,/And drunk the milk of paradise." . . . when there came a knock at the door. Coleridge himself then related what happened. He "unfortunately was called out by a person on business from Porlock, and detained by him for above an hour, and on his return to his room, found, to his no small surprise and mortification, that with the exception of some eight or ten scattered lines and images, all the rest had passed away." The poem ends abruptly at the point where he laid down his pen to answer the knock. By an untimely interruption the remainder was lost forever.

Both you and I can sympathize with Coleridge, for haven't we been bothered by countless interruptions of every size and pedigree? My reaction is, "Yes, poor fellow, I know how he must have felt. 'Persons from Porlock' are

calling on *me* all the time!" How often such interruptions
seem to shunt us from the main track onto a siding.

We may think this, but "'taint necessarily so!" You will
remember the Old Testament patriarch who wanted to serve
God so devotedly that he built an altar, stoked it with wood,
bound the hands and feet of his young son, laid him as a
sacrificial animal on the altar, and tremblingly raised the
knife. Abraham had to believe strongly that he was on the
main track to go through with a deed like that! But there
came an interruption. An angel cried, "Hold on! Do not
harm the lad." When Abraham looked around, he saw a ram
caught in a thicket by his horns.

It was an interruption which saved Isaac's life—an interruption important to the spiritual growth of the Hebrew
people. For through it, *Abraham learned that his whole thinking
about God thus far had been on a siding!* Now God was shoving
him out onto the main, double-tracked line which was to
lead directly, centuries later, to the stirring cry of Micah:
"What does the Lord require of you/but to do justice and
to love kindness,/and to walk humbly with your God?"
(Mic. 6-8). By means of an interruption, a vital spiritual
truth was introduced to humankind.

The same thing may happen in our own day. Some of the
interruptions which plague you and me are related to the
health of our spirits. Consider the kind we abhor. A woman
is mixing a golden-glow cake when the doorbell rings. A
salesman wants to take magazine subscriptions. A man is
pushing office work which must be done that afternoon,
when his wife telephones that she must have a pair of hose
before the stores close.

Or consider how welcome interruptions can be unwholesome. A housewife is at a desk unsuccessfully attempting to write an urgent but difficult letter when the step
of the mail carrier is heard on the porch. Or here is a man

cornered in his own home by the minister—a most deplorable situation! "We've been missing you the past six months," the minister begins briskly, and, as the man shrinks in his chair, the wife makes a blessed entry, bubbling over with the phenomenal success of the recent rubbish sale. For the rest of the day this man is extra kind to his wife in gratitude for her timely intervention. Welcome interruptions—both of these—but not necessarily wholesome.

What I need to remind myself is that both welcome and unwelcome interruptions can be either angelic or demonic. This means that unwelcome ones can come from God. *For I believe that there are occasions when God Himself deliberately fashions the interruptions of your life and mine.* In God's purposes they become instruments by which His will is accomplished in our daily living.

Perhaps it may seem revolutionary to you that God at times may upset your life. As you remember some of the interruptions, the bigger wrecks along the main track of your life, you recall the cost in blood, sweat, and tears, and think, *Surely God did not will me* that! But you and I do well to include the big interruptions as well. Why is this desirable?

In the days following the resurrection, many persons were converted to belief in Jesus. Much havoc was wrought in the early church by Saul, a gifted but ruthless Pharisee. Regarding Christians as traitors of the worst sort, Saul was "ravaging the church, and entering house after house, he dragged off men and women and committed them to prison" (Acts 8:3). Then hearing that Christians had turned up in Damascus, he secured extradition papers and headed for Syria, "still breathing threats and murder against" them (9:1).

But we know that God interrupted that journey, turning topsy-turvy Saul's mind and heart. God seized this man who knew so passionately that he was right, broke him into little pieces, shook them around, and put them together in a new pattern: Saint Paul! The church can thank God, literally, for that interruption.

Sometimes, then, it takes a major revolution before God can shake you and me loose from second-rate ideals or undesirable habits to which we so stubbornly cling. It is a major interruption *when we are moved from the siding where we may love to sit over on to the main tracks where God wants us to travel.* Sometimes we might declare that God is destroying our usefulness, when actually He is moving us relentlessly toward some turning point He knows we must experience.

This means, doesn't it, that you and I must examine each interruption with care, to determine if it's from God. The more firmly we are set in thoughts and habits, the greater the likelihood of a Divine Interruption. In reacting to "persons from Porlock" or accident, illness, loss of employment, or whatnot, we have the same choices that a draft horse in trouble does: we can whinny piteously, we can kick out and become tangled in the harness, we can stand idle rebelliously in the traces, we can dash madly away in all directions, or we can try to understand what is going on and patiently help the process along.

So we must ask of each major interruption, "Are you from God?" If indeed God has sent it—and it may be in unusual disguise—you and I must accept it and conform our lives to its demands. *And the less it looks to be from God, the more carefully must we scrutinize it!* For sometimes God can enter our lives only through a major revolution. In prayerful mood we shall ask, "What do You want me to learn, Father? Where must I change my life? Toward what now-hidden goal are You urging me?" The more disturbing the trouble, the more thorough should be our search to find the hidden purposes of God.

Of course, there are times when an interruption might not be God's call but simply a human misfortune such as a crippling accident, a wasting illness, or an untimely death. What can you and I do when we are indeed shunted off to such a siding? I have found it heartening to remember that *even though God may not have initiated that interruption and did not forestall it, yet He is still present in that unfortunate experience, with power to help.* Through His strength I can turn that interruption into a spiritual achievement. Paul testified to this truth when he wrote: "We are afflicted in every way, but not crushed; perplexed, but not driven to despair; persecuted, but not forsaken; struck down, but not destroyed" (2 Cor. 4:8-9).

Genesis tells us that Jacob once wrestled with an angel who dislocated the patriarch's thigh. The angel then said, "Let me go, for day is breaking." But Jacob, now recognizing the nature of his assailant, replied stubbornly, "I will not let you go until you bless me!" (Gen. 32:26, VV).

Isn't this a secret to use whenever we wrestle with any distressing interruption? Jesus used it on the cross. Similarly, rather than drawing back in anguish and self-pity, you and I can tenaciously seize hold of our trouble and affirm, "Through God's power you're going to do me good. I'm coming out of this stronger than I went in. Evil though you may seem to be, you're going to bless me!"

Thus, as we learn to handle interruptions in this aggressive fashion, they will offer unexpected dividends.

I can do all things in him who strengthens me (Phil. 4:13).

20.
Learn How to Throw Temptations Down the Stairs

Count it all joy, my brethren, when you meet various trials, for you know that the testing of your faith produces steadfastness. And let steadfastness have its full effect, that you may be perfect and complete (Jas. 1:2-4).

The story goes that a saintly Huguenot named Jean-Pierre once lived in a small garret off a back street in the cathedral town of Bourges. One of his admirers was a timid street sweeper. This man was pushing his loaded cart toward the dump when the right wheel struck a high cobblestone, and the rubbish was scattered. "The devil take it!" he exclaimed in vexation.

No sooner had he spoken than the refuse utterly disappeared. While the man stared at his overturned cart in stupefaction, he became aware of a shadowy, red-cloaked figure materializing at his elbow whose leering, crafty face was topped by a neat pair of curling horns. A great fear seized the sweeper, and dropping to his knees, he drew in the dust the sign of the Cross.

The devil looked down at him sardonically. "I have just done you a favor. Perhaps you will now do one for me."

"Ah, no! Jean-Pierre has told me many times to have no dealings with Satan."

The devil's brow darkened. "Jean-Pierre! That pious hypocrite! He's always getting in my way, just as that cobblestone got in your way." Tiny lightnings flashed in the hooded eyes. "Methinks I will pay this Jean-Pierre a visit.

And as for you, miserable creature, creep back to your hovel and your bowl of boiled parsnips, and trouble me no more!" With that, the devil vanished.

With trembling knees the sweeper righted his empty cart and hastened to his cottage where he poured out the dreadful adventure to his wife. "Poor Jean-Pierre," he exclaimed over and over again. "Satan has taken his soul."

After tossing restlessly for much of the night, and being tortured by imagining in gruesome detail a dozen different fates for the saint, the sweeper arose at dawn and hastened to Jean-Pierre's chamber. Climbing the rickety outside staircase, and dreading what he might find, the sweeper burst into the room without pausing to knock. And there at his kneeling-bench was Jean-Pierre, hands folded in prayer. At the interruption Jean-Pierre turned an unruffled countenance which quite bewildered the sweeper. "Good morning, my friend."

Mouth fallen open, the sweeper gaped at him speechlessly for a moment and then cried, "Are you . . . are you all right?"

"Quite all right, thank you," replied the saint serenely.

"But last night the devil told me he was coming for your soul!"

Jean-Pierre nodded. "Yes, he came."

"What . . . what happened?"

Jean-Pierre smiled quietly. "The moment I knew who he was, I called on the name of the Lord and threw the devil down the stairs."

"You did!"

"Yes. It happened to him in heaven once, you know, and I was just following the Almighty's example."

Here is one guideline in our quest for victorious living: *Never for one moment leave the devil in doubt as to what his reception will be!* Never are we to let him get a foothold in our door! Nor is it ever safe to open the door just a crack to get a good look at him, for he is a mighty persuasive salesman. I know! The only surefire method of handling him is Jean-Pierre's. The apostle James knew this technique: "Resist the devil and he will flee from you. Draw near to God and he will draw near to you" (Jas. 4:7).

I believe in *the demonic,* because I have seen the devil at work in people, and sometimes I even feel the insidious stirring within my own life. The truth is dreadful—namely, that the demonic is already within humankind.

A demon, then, attempts evilly to possess you or me, even though a demon cannot possess those of us in Christ. A demon would change us from free souls directing our lives toward God's holy purposes, toward becoming shackled slaves whose powers are turned in the wrong direction. When we have succeeded in throwing such temptations and impulses down the stairs, like persistent cats they keep creeping back up, crouching in wait till we incautiously open the door again. We dare not, then, grow tired of ridding ourselves of temptations in Jean-Pierre's forthright fashion, lest we forfeit our earlier victories.

Even though these demons cannot possess us, how do they give evidence of their presence? They are found in *occasional dishonesties* wherein we are not quite truthful, either with ourselves or with those about us; in *flashes of irritability* when we have been thwarted in our desires or have been discovered in some less-than-honorable pursuit; in our *secret conceits* which lead us to think too highly of ourselves and too contemptuously of others.

Additional demons are found in our *continuing indifference* to noble causes which demand that we give of our best: our home, our church, a wholesome educational system, sound and compassionate government, and a world organized on principles of brotherhood and justice, rather than on hatred and greed. And demons manifest themselves in our *insistent hungers* for greater wealth, whose quest may lead to gambling or financial trickery; for *unwholesome love,* whose search may result in license or lust; for *desire for attention,* which may lead to profanity or deliberately shocking behavior; for *unnatural stimulation,* which may lead to addiction to alcohol, nicotine, or drug abuse.

Oh, there are ways too numerous to catalogue for detecting the presence of demons. And there is only one sure-fire means of evicting them: the formula of Jean-Pierre. In his autobiography, *The Making of an Insurgent,* the late mayor of New York, Fiorello LaGuardia wrote:

> When I was first assigned to Night Court, Andrew Tedesco of the Immigration Service said to me, "You can get experience on this job, or you can make a great deal of money. I don't think you'll take the money. But remember that the test is if you hesitate. Unless you say no right off, the first time an offer comes your way, you are gone."
> I always remembered that bit of advice through my career. It was the first instinctive reaction against dishonesty or indecency that always counted, and I have repeated Tedesco's advice to many men entering public service where they are subject to temptation.[4]

Even Jesus found this to be true, particularly facing the temptations epitomized in His wilderness experience. There He was tempted (a) to use his marvelous powers for His own personal ends, (b) to use wrong means to achieve right ends, and (c) to use His powers spectacularly to attract followers. The record declares that Jesus resisted them all on the tempter's first proposition, yet Luke states that when the devil had ended every temptation, he departed from Him "for a season" (v. 13, KJV), or in a newer translation, "until an opportune time." He would be back later! But it did the devil no good, for each time any temptation came—even when in agony on the cross—Jesus immediately "threw him down the stairs."

Every so often I give myself a word of warning. I cannot throw anything down the stairs to be rid of it, if I am already living in the basement! Otherwise, it would end up right in my living room. That is, *you and I must be living above life's cellar level before we can properly dispose of temptations.* Thus Jesus told His disciples bluntly, "Watch and pray that you may not enter into temptation" (Matt. 26:41).

The old Frenchman, Jean-Pierre, has told us what we need to know. His was a simple, three-pronged technique:

(a) the very moment Jean-Pierre, recognized the temptation for what it was,

(b) he called on the name of the Lord for strength, and

(c) cast out that temptation headlong.

In this age of ultrapersuasive advertising, made insidious by psychological and subliminal gimmicks designed to increase our appetites subconsciously, many temptations are too powerful for your unaided strength and mine. So the next time any demonic temptation confronts us, however skillfully camouflaged, we can meet it without hesitation. And with the name of God on our lips, we can reveal that we are the spiritual kin of Jean-Pierre.

Here is one of the more dramatic means of learning how to master life!

Blessed is the man who endures trial, for when he has stood the test he will receive the crown of life which God promises to those who love him (Jas. 1:12).

21.
Develop the Power of Perseverance

Pray at all times in the Spirit, with all prayer and supplication; to that end keep alert with all perseverance (Eph. 6:18).

On a mission station in India a nine-year-old boy kept pestering his parents and other staff members for a watch. The begging and pleading went on day after day till the father finally warned sternly, "Andy Hume, if you ask anyone for a watch once more, I shall have to punish you."

So for a whole day blessed peace reigned throughout the station. The next morning the missionary families gathered for morning devotions, each answering to a roll call with a verse of Scripture. When Andy's turn came, with cherubic innocence he repeated Jesus' admonition, out of context: "What I say unto you I say unto all: Watch!" Inasmuch as Andy's father was not an inhumane legalist but possessed a saving humor, he ultimately quoted Pilate's words to the chief priests, also out of context: "Ye [may] have a watch" (Matt. 27:65, KJV).

Here is a story of perseverance. Unless you and I possess what my mother called "stick-to-it-iveness," we gain little lasting satisfaction in life. Indeed, wasn't Andy right in using Scripture for persevering as he did, for there are numerous biblical instances of persons who succeeded in doing God's will only after keeping at it again and again through failure and disappointment? Hebrews reminds us that

"God's promise was at last fulfilled because Abraham patiently persevered" (Heb. 6:15, VV).

Jesus told a parable about a widow whose property had
been stolen by a con man. This happened often because
there was an "open season" on widows and orphans; and
Jesus once lashed out against the Scribes "who devour widows' houses and for a pretense make long prayers" (Mark
12:40). But this widow took her complaint to a judge who,
unfortunately, "had no fear of God and no respect for
humanity." Being intent on feathering his own nest, the
judge made no pretense of meeting the needs of indigent
people. But she was made of stern stuff and decided to wear
him down. She kept after him whenever he appeared at
court, when he was going to and from his house, and when
he was eating in restaurants or chatting in the marketplace.
She persistently demanded justice, and she did not believe
in whispering! Finally, irritated beyond measure and nagged
by his friends, the judge said to himself, "Because this
widow bothers me, I will vindicate her, or she will wear me
out by her continual coming" (Luke 18:2-5).

Perseverance alone turned the trick. Never would that
widow have received her property had she not stuck to her
campaign—repugnant though it may have been to her—
with all the gluey persistence she possessed. And how is life
any different today? Neither you nor I can reach out lan-
guidly and pluck without effort the "fruit of the Spirit" or
anything else of authentic value. Not at all! Ever since Adam
and Eve became displaced persons, we descendants have had
to win all our fruits by the sweat of our brows. *There is no such
thing as extemporaneous human grandeur.* The things we prize the
most are those over which someone has toiled and agonized.
Sam Coles used to put it like this: "The thing that doesn't
hurt in its getting has little value."

The standard American history textbook at the turn of the

century was one written by George Bancroft—after he had spent twenty-six years in its preparation. Gibbon worked more than twenty years on his monumental *Decline and Fall of the Roman Empire.* Thomas Gray did not dash off his "Elegy Written in a Country Churchyard" on the backs of envelopes during those moments when waiting for his wife to put on her hat! The British Museum owns seventy-five different drafts of that poem, representing the number of times Gray made a fresh start at it in the hope of recording precisely what was in his heart. Ignace Jon Paderewski amazed the world for forty years as a classical pianist, not so much because he was a musical genius but because he practiced as much as seventeen hours a day. Thus, it is vital for you and me to remember that grandeur to which we may aspire is not extemporaneous, but hard-won. This is particularly true in the religious arena. Except for salvation, God reserves His best gifts for those who earn them through faithful perseverance.

I believe that *this power to persevere is a capacity which God loans to us as a part of our marching equipment.* For just as this trait pays off in writing, painting, playing a violin, or in making a living, so it also pays off in the holy areas of our existence. In his little classic, *The Greatest Thing in the World,* Henry Drummond asks, "What makes a man a good musician? Practice. What makes a man a good linguist? A good stenographer? Practice. What makes a man a good man? Practice, nothing else. If a man does not exercise his arm he develops no biceps muscle; if a man does not exercise his soul, he acquires no muscle in his soul, no strength of character, no vigor of moral fiber, no beauty of spiritual growth." Rugged character shaped after the fashion of Jesus is the crowning adornment of your life and mine, and we win it only by the exercise of every ounce of perseverance we can muster. "If we have died with [Christ]," Paul wrote Timothy, "we shall also live with him; if we endure, we shall also reign with him" (2 Tim. 2:11-12).

Forty-five years ago in the *Atlantic Monthly,* Arthur Kudner told how he had seen a pair of cowboys bring to the ranch a steer which had long been in the wilds. With them they took a diminutive burro. "Now," related Kudner,

> a big three-year-old steer that's been running loose in the timber is a tough customer to handle. But these cowboys had the right technique. They got a rope on the steer and then they tied him neck-and-neck right up close, to the burro. Then the cowboys returned to the ranch.
>
> When they let go, that burro had a bad time. The steer threw him all over the place. He banged him against trees, rocks, into bushes. Time after time they went down. But there was one great difference between the burro and the steer—the burro had an idea. He wanted to go home. And no matter how often the steer threw him, every time the burro got to his feet, he took a step nearer the corral. This went on and on. After about a week the burro showed up at the ranch. He had with him the tamest and sorriest-looking steer you ever saw!

Isn't this a modern version of the parable of the unjust judge? Isn't it also a parable which indicates that as you and I increase our power of perseverance in our discipleship, nothing on earth can keep us from one day reaching our eternal home!

> Since we are surrounded by so great a cloud of witnesses, let us lay aside every weight, and sin which clings so closely, and let us run with perseverance the race that is set before us, looking to Jesus the pioneer and perfecter of our faith (Heb. 12:1-2).

22.
Deepen the Root of a Patient Spirit

[God] will render to every man according to his works: to those who by patience
in well-doing seek for glory and honor and immortality, he will give eternal life
(Rom. 2:6-7).

During the period of the Civil War, James Truslow Adams
told us, impatience became a common trait of the American
people. "All observers of the period note the new haste with
which Americans gulped down their meals and hurried from
the table. The American jaws began their ceaseless motion."
Another historian, describing the New Englander, wrote:

> When his feet are not in motion, his fingers must be in action;
> he must be whittling a piece of wood, cutting the back of his
> chair or notching the end of the table; or his jaws must be
> grinding tobacco. He always has something to be done, he is
> always in a terrible hurry. He is fit for all sorts of work except
> that which requires slow, minute processes.

Another American of that day commented: "We are born in
haste, we finish our education on the run, we marry on the
wing, we make a fortune at a stroke and lose it in the same
manner."

Don't these early American characteristics aptly describe
the tone of today's culture? Impatience is nothing new in our
national memory, for we have never been a patient people.
If you and I are to find for ourselves the art of patience, we
must learn what sort of root it requires, and how to send that

root deeply into the subsoil of our lives. Although numbers of small adventitious roots might be named, we shall consider only the main taproot—*our integration of mind and heart which produces inward purity—a self-integration around a single-minded devotion to God.* In the sixth Beatitude this quality is defined: "Congratulations to those whose motives are pure, for they will enter the very presence of God" (Matt. 5:8, VV).

In his book *The Life and Death of a Spanish Village,* Elliott Paul described one of the individuals who haunted the granite ledges along the seashore. Nicknamed "the Admiral," he had "long, unkempt hair and beard, both of which he shaved clean once a year in midsummer. He laughed, grinned and talked to himself when alone. I have heard him walking home drunk in the brightest moonlight carrying on a reproachful and defensive conversation aloud, one voice in Spanish, the other in French, sometimes softly and persuasively, often reaching an angry crescendo so that the two of his selves would be bellowing at each other."

Sometimes you and I are in the same boat with the admiral! Charlotte Elliott described our predicament when she wrote the hymn:

> Just as I am, though tossed about
> With many a conflict, many a doubt,
> Fightings within and fears without.

Here is a description of the way I can be at war with myself. At such times, inconsequential events can rub me the wrong way; I can become extra sensitive to little irritants which normally I would brush aside, and my ability to stand up to punishment weakens. Then it becomes difficult indeed for me to possess my soul in patience. When I am inwardly disunited, I do not know how to meet life's buffetings creatively.

If you are a parent you know firsthand how contagious

any impatience you show may become. If you return home in an irritated state, tense with unresolved inner conflicts, you find yourself snapping at the children and growling at your spouse for perfectly nonsensical reasons, till they begin acting the same way themselves.

But when you and I make a personal commitment of our lives to God, putting them under new management, we at once find a center outside self around which we can integrate all living. Allowing no earlier habit or loyalty to adulterate that new commitment, we will be observing the First Commandment: "You shall have no other gods before me" (Ex. 20:3). Thus we gather up and unify all the drives and motivations that heretofore have pushed us in conflicting or unChristlike directions. Then we become, not a combination of fractured parts, but whole persons, inwardly and outwardly unified individuals with uncontaminated purity of heart. And when we as whole persons greet our families, we have such a grip on ourselves that whatever may happen— whether Jimmy totals the car or the company stock drops seven points—we can meet with equanimity and humor. We become invulnerable to irritations because we are no longer beset by the fear that life is gradually going to pieces and that any tiny speck will hasten the catastrophe. *For we learn to hold ourselves together in the face of normally disruptive experiences.* The psalmist exulted, "Great peace have those who love thy law; nothing can make them stumble" (Ps. 119:165).

Robert Ingersoll, the cocky agnostic of the past century, once spent an hour publicly deriding Christianity. At the end of his talk Ingersoll took out his watch, laid it on the lectern, and said, "I'll give God five minutes to strike me dead for the things I've said." In dramatic silence he watched as the time ticked off while the audience waited in suspense. Nothing happened, of course. The newspapers gave the event big headlines, but one thoughtful citizen commented drily, "Did he think he could exhaust the patience of God in five minutes?"

This incident is worth remembering. God is infinitely patient with you and me—perverse and thickheaded children that sometimes we are! For

> He has not treated us as our sins deserve or requited us for our misdeeds.
> For as the heaven stands high above the earth, so his strong love stands high over all who fear him (Ps. 103:10-11, NEB).

God is patient because He possesses the inward unity which we are to exemplify: "The Lord our God, the Lord is one" (Deut. 6:4, KJV)

As we gain comparable inward unity through total commitment to God, we will find the roots of a patient spirit.

> Have no anxiety about anything, but in everything by prayer and supplication with thanksgiving let your requests be made known to God. And the peace of God, which passes all understanding, will keep your hearts and minds in Christ Jesus (Phil. 4:6-7).

23.
Learn to Sing in Your Darkness

Let the faithful exult in glory; let them sing for joy on their couches. Let the high praises of God be in their throats (Ps. 149:5-6).

Some time ago I spent a week in the surgical ward of a Florida hospital. Becoming ambulatory, I took to prowling the corridors. Late one night I passed a partly-closed door through which came the sound of soft singing. I paused, listened for a moment, and then recognized the hymn: "O Thou Who changest not, abide with me!" My heart warmed toward that unknown soul who, lonely, fearful, or pain ridden, was hungry for sleep which did not come but nevertheless was dauntlessly expressing her faith.

My memory was jogged, and I returned to my room to examine my Bible. For didn't Paul and Silas know about singing hymns at midnight? Sure enough, these men were railroaded to prison after being beaten. Yet Luke wrote, "About midnight Paul and Silas were praying and singing hymns to God, and the prisoners were listening to them" (Acts 16:25).

Here were similar situations: one in a modern hospital and the other in an ancient prison, separated only by some nineteen-hundred years. What underlay this expression of Paul and Silas's faith? Following an inner call, Paul had gone to Troas on the Eastern shore of the Aegean Sea, beyond which, to the west, stretched Europe—as yet untouched by

121

the message of Jesus. There Paul had a vision of a man standing on the far shore, pleading, "Come over and give us the good news of Jesus!" Here was a divine commission to evangelize not just the Jewish people but everyone in the world. I can picture Paul and Silas's enthusiasm as they trudged the weary miles to Philippi. There no one paid attention to them till Paul healed an enslaved, clairvoyant girl, and she lost her powers to foretell the future. Her angry owners trumped up charges which caused Paul and Silas to be beaten with rods and chained in a dungeon. What a sudden and shocking end to their high hopes! *They knew the midnight which comes from the bitter despair of defeated expectations.*

And sometimes, so do we! Haven't we known high moments of devotion to lofty ideals and then found, with a sinking sense of dismay, that our hopes were going down the drain? Or just at the height of some cherished quest, we have found ourselves bound hand and foot by our own forgotten limitations, or imprisoned by the unwitting obstructions of circumstances. Then our sails have lost their wind, and we sit becalmed in an ocean of frustration.

But this was not the reaction of Paul and Silas to their miseries. They sang hymns of praise, right out loud. So can we. Their prison doors eventually were opened. So also can ours.

Our "midnights" can come in many varieties and styles, for there are times when we share with the missionaries the bitter despair of defeated expectations. One of America's great pulpiteers once told about a woman who in her youth revealed outstanding artistic ability in many areas, but her major passion was music. Possessing a rich contralto voice, she studied for three years in Italy and France, then returned to this country with high hopes of a career in opera. But a smooth, reputable professional man wooed her expertly, and they were married. Then with sadistic selfishness, cloaked with an outwardly deferential manner, he subjected this singing spirit to almost insufferable tyranny. Restrictions were inflicted with honeyed words at one moment, and persecutions with vicious insinuations at another. Her career was destroyed, and she suffered his cruelty beyond the call of duty. At last, the husband died, cutting her out of his will. Today, having never realized her expectations, she supports herself and her growing children by giving voice lessons.

Recently this lady wrote to a friend, telling her life story which is full of shadows and frustrations. One might expect the outpourings of an anguished soul, but she wrote without complaint. At the end, she added one sentence which is the hallmark of her indomitable spirit: "Actually, I have done one thing on this earth: I have continued to sing!" Undoubtedly, it was a song more often in the heart than on the lips. But she knew the truth of the Psalm: "By day the Lord commands his steadfast love; and at night his song is with me" (Ps. 42:8). She took the psalmist at his word. Out of the blackness of her woe there came songs of victory—hymns at midnight which opened prison doors.

Now, you and I may at times face the danger of being overtaken by hate, either arising within us or being directed against us. The Philippian merchants had the missionaries jailed because they hated them—not just because their lucrative exploitation of a helpless girl had been ended but also because the newcomers were Jews; therefore, they were regarded as perennial troublemakers. Ethnic and racial prejudice was a contributing cause of their "midnight"—a brooding blackness which nineteen centuries later has hardly been diminished. I have visited the former Nazi concentration camp at Dachau near Munich, seeing the barracks and punishment rooms, the so-called "shower rooms" whose shower heads spouted lethal gas, and the crematory ovens which were Hitler's "final answer to the Jewish prob-

124 Coping Is Not Enough

lem." And I also recollect that during World War II the
United States opened detainment camps for another sud-
denly-hated people on the West Coast, those of Japanese
ancestry.

Now, the hatred of the ordinary Frenchman for the ordinary German has persisted for generations. Yet, during that
vast midnight labeled World War II, there were persons and
groups within each country who were able to sing of recon-
ciliation and forgiveness. Through two trips to both coun-
tries I have learned that those midnight hymns have effected
a remarkable reversal of attitude on both sides of the common border. In my wildest dreams I never would have pic-
tured such friendliness ever being possible. What has
happened indicates that peace is possible between peoples
when enough of them irradiate the midnights of hatred with
hymns of forgiveness.

Other threatening midnights arise from a thousand fears
which shut out the sunlight and create depression and
gloom. There are times when we experience fear for our
bodies—when the possibility of our dying suddenly escapes
from our subconscious and begins to bedevil us. But as has
been suggested, a hospital is a fine place to hold a hymn sing.
Here is Arthur Hewitt's story.

"The November twilight was darkening in the Deaconess
Hospital. In one corner was a man whose terrifying symp-
toms no physician had yet diagnosed. Beside him was one
who must go under the surgeon's knife in the morning.
Diagonally across from my bed was a man shadowed by the
hallucination that he was accused of murder. Every one of
us was in deepest gloom. I had never been in a hospital
before. What malignant thing might be maiming me I did
not know. 'The night was dark, and I was far from home.' "

It was twilight outside the hospital but midnight within
the ward.

"Suddenly," Hewitt continued, "came a chord, a hush, and then a jubilant full chorus from the place where the corridors cross. The nurses had gathered for evensong, and they sang the favorite hymn of my mother, 'He Leadeth Me.' On those voices, God came into the ward!"

Out of the blackness of physical dread a song of faith arose—a hymn at midnight which opened Hewitt's "prison doors."[5]

Thus, whatever fears, dislikes, or bitter disappointments may be creating midnights for us, none of them can survive the purging power of a great hymn. And I mean more than simply figurative hymn singing wherein we summon up attitudes of confidence and trust. I also mean the actual use of the hymnbook where you and I will find hymns to dispel our particular midnights! Raise your voice like that of the Florida patient, and let those hymns jubilantly sound forth!

For we grow in faith as we learn to sing in our darknesses.

> I waited patiently for the Lord;
> he inclined to me and heard my cry.
> He drew me up from the desolate pit,
> out of the miry bog,
> and set my feet upon a rock,
> making my steps secure.
> He put a new song in my mouth,
> a song of praise to our God (Ps. 40:1-3).

24.
Will Yourself to Be Happy

I have learned, in whatever state I am, to be content. I know how to be abased, and I know how to abound; in any and all circumstances I have learned the secret of facing plenty and hunger, abundance and want (Phil. 4:11-13).

In a book describing his childhood on the South Dakota prairie, Hamlin Garland made this poignant observation about his pioneer mother: "So little happiness came to her in one large piece that she was always making her pleasures out of many odds and ends of things." Even though life was extremely difficult for this hardy woman, her life was not without joy. She set her mind toward happiness, and, using her quilting ability, she created it by pure force of will! What an example!

Perhaps she took her cue from Jesus, "who for the joy that was set before him endured the cross, despising the shame" (Heb. 12:2). It is an exceptional person who can face with joy the rough times of life. But we can do it because happiness does not depend on health or wealth, influence or fame, but on our ability, like Mrs. Garland's, to do "piece work" to bring it into existence.

Jesus' family, for example, stood near the bottom of Israel's economic ladder. At first glance, there is little reason why Jesus' life should have been marked with happiness at all. His country had been conquered and occupied by Roman legions. Taxes were staggering and were collected relentlessly. The ruling class, the Sanhedrin with its upper

echelon of priests, had largely sold out to the Romans, and
the earlier vigorous Jewish faith had been largely replaced
by ceremony and ritual. When Jesus began His ministry, it
was first without the endorsement of the Establishment;
then later, with its secret enmity. Indeed, by present stan-
dards there would be little room in Jesus' life for authentic
happiness. But His joy did not arise out of economic security
or social standing, or even out of His friendship for the poor
and the outcast. When He died, His only possessions were
the clothes He wore, and He had to be laid in a borrowed
tomb. Yet although He was "a man of sorrows, and acquainted with grief," he also had the capacity to transmute
despair into victory, sadness into confidence, unhappiness
into joy. *An inward radiance arising from His faith in His Father
enabled Him to set His will toward happiness.*

A ranking tennis star of a previous generation, Helen
Wills Moody, once wrote,

> When as a child I was asked what I would rather have than
> anything else in the world, I would answer, 'a wishing ring,'
> because then I could wish for everything else. But now I
> would ask for an understanding mind, for that would be in
> truth a wishing ring. It must surely be the source of happi-
> ness, for where can happiness arise except in the recesses of
> our own minds?

The late tennis star touched on a vital factor in any search
for happiness. A famous rose grower once declared that he
found his encouragement for his lifework from a sentence
he once read: "Before you can grow beautiful roses in a
greenhouse, you must have beautiful roses in your mind."
And this applies both to you and me. We can be happy
because we will to be happy, resolutely squirreling away
little stocks of it. "I saw that there is nothing better,"
said the Preacher, "than that a man should enjoy his work"

(Eccl. 3:22). Our degree of happiness, then, is not based on what fortunate or unfortunate things happen to us but is founded on our conviction that God knows our need and is concerned enough to come to our aid. Believing this frees our minds from competing worry and distrust, enabling us to will ourselves happiness even in the most unlikely circumstances.

In his *Memoirs*, E. F. Benson described Lady Sandhurst, the daughter of Matthew Arnold, as follows:

> The surface of life never lost its brightness for her. She had her share of sorrows. But she found 'treats' everywhere, small entrancing surprises; the conduct of the ducks on the Serpentine when she took walks in Hyde Park; a barrel-organ with one leg and a red-coated monkey sitting on top, huskily performing "The Lost Chord," the changing of the guard at Buckingham Palace, the changing of traffic lights. She had the genuine Jane Austen eye. Whether she directed it to barrel-organs or bombs, she saw with that uniquely humorous perception.

Exactly!

Thus the power to "pursue happiness"—all that the Declaration of Independence allows!—comes mainly through our exercise of the will. As Paul advised, we are to dwell only on those parts of our daily experience which are true and just, honorable and lovely, pure and of good repute. Whatever is ugly or false, dishonest or corrupting, must be taken sensible note of, and then resolutely put from our minds. *If we will, the troubles we meet need not affect our happiness so long as we do not let them gain dominion over us.*

The encouraging thing about this guideline is: like the others, it also works! Not only is it a source of happiness but also of inward strength. Jesus was able to endure the cross because of joy-given strength. Are you familiar with the pledge which that gifted black author and poet, James Weldon Johnson, sought to keep through the years of his abuse at the hands of whites less educated and cultured than he:

> I will not allow one prejudiced person or one million or one hundred million to blight my life. I will not let prejudice or any of its attendant humiliations and injustices bear me down to spiritual defeat. My inner life is mine, and I shall defend and maintain its integrity against all the powers of hell!

When you and I will ourselves to be happy with this determination, we will find the necessary ingredients for a "continuous quilting party" in each day's living.

While I was a student at Hartford Theological Seminary, a new chapel was being built at Trinity College. One day a workman came to install the stained glass and saw a small, circular window being filled with clear glass because there was not enough money for stained glass there. On returning to the studio, with the permission of the master craftsman, the man gathered up scraps of stained glass about the shop: leftover bits too small to be reclaimed. With infinite patience, he leaded them together into a small rose window, in the center of which shone a cross, and brought it to the chapel as his personal contribution.

Let this serve as a parable of how you and I may win the most enduring happiness. We do not stumble into it; we do not buy it or receive it at the hands of some generous friend. Rather, we shape it purposefully out of many different sources. It comes to us in the same fashion as it came to Jesus—as we set our wills to be happy.

> May you be strengthened with all power, according to his glorious might, for all endurance and patience with joy, giving thanks to the Father, who has qualified us to share in the inheritance of the saints in light (Col. 1:11-12).

25.
Get Yourself Off
Your Hands

As for me, I would seek God,
and to God would I commit my cause;
who does great things and unsearchable,
marvelous things without number (Job 5:8-9).

A physician once told me he had recently said to a patient, "I cannot find a thing organically wrong with you. You can be your own physician by sitting loose to your worries." Isn't this what the psalmist was saying?

Fret not thyself because of evildoers,
    neither be thou envious against the workers of iniquity.
. . .
Commit thy way unto the Lord; trust also in him,
    and he will bring it to pass (Ps. 37:1-5, KJV).

The psalmist intimated, "Get yourself off your hands!" and this is a sound guideline for us. Much of the time our hands are rather full of ourselves. We know moments when, in response to tensions or pressures, we may become

—*discontented* with some part of our daily round;
—*fractious* with those with whom we disagree;
—*petulant* when we are outvoted;
—*touchy* about what we feel are personal matters;
—*impatient* under inescapable duties;
—*vexed* with certain neighbors;
—*jealous* of those who get along better than we do;

—*anxious* about future events;
—*vengeful* against those whom we feel have harmed us.

Have I omitted any?

Now, any one of these is problem enough, so when you or I get two or more of them simultaneously, they can become a staggering load, putting heavy strain on our character and driving both joy and satisfaction from life. Perhaps, then, in our hearts we cry out, "Oh, what can I do? This is not what life ought to be!" So, the doctor's advice can be a useful guideline. *We are to learn how to get ourselves off our hands.*

Right away I must emphasize that this does not mean we are to drop ourselves kerplunk onto somebody else's hands. Here is a temptation to be identified promptly and then thrown down the stairs. I expressed this danger once in these lines entitled "The Old Adam":

> Though trouble prone was Si McCann,
> His days plumb filled with strife,
> He took his troubles like a man—
> He blamed them on his wife!

And it is no kindlier to Si to change the quatrain to read, "He dropped them on his wife"—or on anyone else! Individuals sometimes go to a doctor or minister, counselor or social worker, and confess in effect, "I'm so tired of holding myself. Take me for a while, please!" Of course, both you and I have known in times of emergency a wondrous sense of release when we have turned for help to someone we trust and have found immediate support. Yet while we can share our burden with them, we cannot dump our whole load on them and think, *That's their worry now!* It simply does not work.

How, then, do you and I effectively get ourselves off our hands? *It is by putting ourselves into God's hands!* When we do this, we will find ourselves wonderfully lightened, like John Bunyan's Pilgrim, leaving in God's keeping the things that trouble us most. This will not result in our escaping from eventually bearing them. Rather, we store them with God, and He gives them back for us to deal with as fast as we— through His strength—build up the needed resources. Through that neither you nor I are dodging responsibility but rather finding a practical way to fulfill it. The common word for this is "self-surrender." Jesus was practicing it when, hanging in agony on the cross, He quoted a line from the psalmist: "[Father], into thy hand I commit my spirit" (Ps. 31:5) *It means that you and I shall consign our entire life to God.* We entrust to His care and keeping our entire beings, the totality of our existence, that is, our hopes and dreams, our joys and worries, our successes and disappointments, our short-range motivations and our long-term goals. "Delight thyself also in the Lord," counseled the psalmist, "and he shall give thee the desires of thine heart. . . . Rest in the Lord, and wait patiently for him." (Ps. 37:4-7 KJV). Here is commitment.

Allen Clark relates that when Dr. John Paton was translating the New Testament into a South Pacific language, he had trouble in finding the local word equivalent to "faith." One day a native teacher entered Dr. Paton's study, hot and exhausted after a long walk from another village. He sank into a cane chair, put his feet up on another chair, and, wiping his forehead, used a word which means, "I am resting my whole weight here." At once Dr. Paton had the word he was searching for. *Faith means resting our whole weight on God day after day.*

Some people exclaim, "But isn't that a cowardly or lazy thing to do—dropping everything you can't handle onto

God? Didn't Jesus say that everyone must bear his or her own burden? Why make God a scapegoat for all your weaknesses and failures?" What balderdash! *Self-surrender is but the sensible fulfilling of our destiny.* The author of Proverbs counseled, "Commit your work to the Lord, and your plans will be established" (Prov. 16:3). This is how we gain the understanding and courage we need for everyday living.

In my childhood, our living room held a wonderful, wide wicker rocking chair. The shape and length of the rockers were such that maximum comfort was gained by tilting back beyond what one normally would think to be the safe limit. One day a diminutive family friend whom we knew as Aunt Edna appeared for a visit. With due ceremony she was placed in the big rocker. Wishing to be hospitable, my father put his hand on the back, leaned on it a bit, and advised, "Now, Edna, just settle back, and you'll find a more comfortable position."

But as she felt herself tipping backward, and her feet coming off the floor, she was beset with visions of going over backward completely in an unseemly flurry of petticoats. So rather than relaxing, she leaned forward desperately, beating a tattoo on the wickerwork with her feet. Not sensing her fear, my father kept pushing the chair further back till it finally settled into the proper, secure position for which it was designed.

"Now, Edna," he counseled, "let yourself go. The chair won't tip any further."

With a nervous little squeal which still echoes in my mind, she cautiously relaxed till she touched the chair back. It seemed perfectly firm, so she eased her deathlike grip on the arms. There was indeed no further tipping, so with a sigh she settled back and let the tenseness drain from her muscles. She began to rest her whole weight there. In a few moments she remarked to my father, "Why, Will, this is the most comfortable chair I've ever sat in. What a pity it's so hard to get into!"

This a little parable about getting ourselves off our hands and onto the Lord's! How often you and I fight against the most exhilarating experience in the world—learning the joy of resting our whole weight on the Lord.

Trust in the Lord and do good
so you will dwell in the land, and enjoy security.
Take delight in the Lord,
and he will give you the desires of your heart.
Commit your way to the Lord;
trust in him, and he will act (Ps. 37:3-5).

26.

Put More Holiness into Sex

I appeal to you therefore, brethren, by the mercies of God, to present your bodies as a living sacrifice, holy and acceptable to God, which is your spiritual worship (Rom. 12:1).

A modern disciple of Jesus accepts all of creation as God's intentional gifts to His children. The roots of this attitude are found in Genesis: "God saw all that he had made, and it was very good" (Gen. 1:31, NEB). Now, the sex relation is an integral part of that creation which God found to be good. He devised and engineered sex into most of His living universe. "Male and female he created them. And God blessed them" (Gen. 1:27-28, NEB). It is a good relationship which God intends to exist between a man and a woman. Wholesome and proper in its essential nature, under the right conditions it is also wholesome and proper for your use and mine.

At times this has been denied. The ascetic transcendentalism of the Middle Ages similarly labeled the sex relation as evil, and more recently, our Puritan forebears must accept some of the blame for perpetuating the same sub-Christian attitude. *All these failed to differentiate between the good things which God created for our use, and the ways in which we human beings ourselves at times have sullied them by obvious misuse.*

For as there are "laws" governing the whole of the physical creation, so also there are "laws" governing the sex relation, that is, *conditions under which it adds to life's wholesomeness and purpose, and conditions under which it destroys that wholesomeness and purpose.* As an engineer uses his knowledge of the manner in which matter reacts to centrifugal and centripetal forces, so as to design a breathtaking roller-coaster in conformity to the laws of gravity, so also you and I may use the sex relation in conformity to its law—to bless both our individual efforts toward self-realization and the concern of both partners for the fulfillment of our corporate identity. When the sex relation is used according to the rules, then it becomes a channel through which the Holy can flow into our lives. God has intended this to be so. Genesis tells us, "God created human beings, male and female, in his own image. . . . And God blessed them, seeing that all his acts were very good" (Gen. 1:27-28,31, VV). *Sex becomes sacred, then, because it becomes a means by which God's outflowing power may reach into the inmost beings of His children, which is a major source of happiness.*

But by the same token, when we use the sex relation in violation of the rules, it ceases to be holy and becomes cheap. Gradually it may tear down the personalities of those who indulge in sex "profanely." Indeed, the misuse of the sex relation can produce all sorts of hells into which an unwary couple can fall, the pleasures so carelessly sought suddenly being exchanged for unwanted pregnancy or disease, or even the hollow experience of being "burned out." The sex mechanism is not at fault but rather the conditions under which it was used.

I believe, then, that you and I can choose to engage either in angelic or demonic sex. Which it shall be is determined by how much holiness we put into it.

There are two separate aspects of the sex relation: procreation and interpersonality bonding. In the *reproductive function,* the sex relation ensures the perpetuation of the race and enables couples to introduce new life, both into the family and the planet. The conception, birth, and rearing of a child

—the process by which God's human agents such as we carry forward His work of creation—is no casual deal in God's eyes. Part of sex's holiness, then, comes from its ability to create new life and personality according to God's will. It is His intention that a child shall come into life through the genuine love of a couple for each other. *That child shall be at once a tangible evidence to society of that love, a dividend of that love to the parents, and a recipient of that love in his or her own life.* When the sex relation is used aright, children will be conceived only under the conditions which God desires, namely an environment of loving welcome and sacrificial dedication which will bless their childhood, guide their youth, and hallow their middle and declining years. This is how it is supposed to work.

This means that sexual intimacies are holy when they occur between a man and a woman who can provide the necessary love, care, and wholesome environment which children require. Children must not be brought, by the whim of an evening's pleasure, into circumstances where they receive less than the minimal opportunity they need to grow according to the divine potential within them. They must not be conceived unless their conception expresses their prospective parents' joyous and permanent sense of mutuality which alone gives the act of reproduction its sacred character. *They must not be brought into a family which does not want them or when a mother's life is imperiled, or when the material resources or family cohesiveness are strained.* Under conditions such as these, doesn't it also become plain that *no child should be conceived outside of marriage by the temporary liaison of two individuals not committed to each other?*

So the sex relation is holy when, under the right conditions, it results in the miracle of conception. This is one of its intended functions. But the relation can also be holy when, under the right conditions and by the mutual consent of the couple, it does not result in the miracle of conception. For there is a second sacred function which is equal to that of procreation and separate from it and which yields a different sort of fruit. It is the function of *interpersonality bonding*. For the sex relation blesses a couple when it binds or fuses them more closely to one another, with or without procreation. It is designed to serve as an instrument for expressing otherwise inexpressible affection, as a channel for communicating the instinct of self-giving love, as a symbol of an increasing intermingling of personalities, as a testament of the utter commitment of each partner toward the other, and as a celebration of the wonder of deepening oneness or togetherness. The sex relation then can serve as a divine tool for enriching personalities and maturing souls, totally apart from procreation.

But there are certain "right conditions."

(1) The sex relation yields its blessings only when it is mutually desired by both parties;

(2) It must not be sought furtively or clandestinely, but as a wholesome, God-given experience which is proper for married couples in love;

(3) It is to be entered into by each partner unselfishly, with the desire to give and to share in a profound experience which outweighs any hunger to seize from the other a bit of self-gratification;

(4) It shall symbolize the joy found in the day-to-day sharing of experiences; and

(5) It shall express, through the act of "becoming one flesh," the deeper unity of mind and spirit into which the couple is growing.

Now, because conditions such as these are required to make the sex relation holy, it is obvious that *the sex relation cannot be holy outside of marriage!* It is only within wedlock that such conditions can make the sex relation a holy instrument of love. If a couple's lives are not entwined, and sex serves only momentarily their self-centered desires for pleasurable self-gratification, then that relationship cannot possibly serve God's purposes. Sex becomes a cheapening, corrosive instrument in their hands.

Sex is holy only when it binds a married couple more closely in mutual love, when it expresses that couple's immediate and long-range oneness of loving purpose, when it serves as an instrument which deepens the personal commitment of one to the other, and when it provides the atmosphere in which the couple comes both to long for a child and to prepare psychologically and financially to receive one. Thus it is that God shares with us the wonder and mystery of His creative power!

You and I grow into spiritual maturity as we commit ourselves fully to the holiness of the sex relation and help others to understand its hallowed nature.

Do you not know that your body is a temple of the Holy Spirit within you, which you have from God? You are not your own; you were bought with a price. So glorify God in your body (1 Cor. 6:19-20).

27.

Acquire Inward Peace by Wading Through

Blessed are the peacemakers, for they shall be called sons of God (Matt. 5:9).

"It is plain today," wrote Herbert Gray, "that the world's supreme need is for men and women of a finer quality, more able to stand the strains of modern life, and to deal efficiently with its challenges without becoming hard or nervous or irritable." Jesus gave the answer to this need when He reassured His disciples, "Peace I leave with you; my peace I give to you; not as the world gives do I give to you. Let not your hearts be troubled, neither let them be afraid" (John 14:27). And yet, as you and I look into the maelstrom of the public world, and inwardly to the windstorm of worries, tensions, and uncertainties which sometimes dominate our private worlds, we honestly wonder whether authentic inner peace is not, after all, purely an illusion.

Many different unproductive efforts are being made in the quest for inward peace. Among these fake nostrums are barbiturates and tranquilizers, alcohol and hallucinogenic drugs, sensual indulgence, the search for wealth, fame, or even distinction in philanthropy or the arts. The essential nature of each of these methods is that of escape. They represent a retreat from the tensions which warp personality, a retreat which sometimes becomes a rout. Just as a pleasure yacht drives frantically ahead of a hurricane to find shelter in a protected bay, so you and I at times are tempted to flee hastily from burdening pressures which menace us. Such tactics may mean safety to a ship, but they can erode our souls. Let us examine a few of these escape routes which no disciple has a moral right to enjoy.

First, there is *beet-like imperturbability.* For some years we had a big garden. While pulling up the last of the beets one fall, I found myself thinking what peaceful vegetables they are. That beet which I held in my hand had not protested when, in seed form, I had dropped it into a shallow trench and threw dirt in its face; it had germinated without excitement and grown without complaint, placidly taking nutrients from soil and sun. Then I pulled it up, and it lay inert, unblinking. It tumbled unresistingly into a basket. My wife would amputate parts of it with her kitchen scalpel, ruthlessly flay its skin with a scrub brush, and then boil it to death in hot water. But nothing in its experience, including that of being eaten, can disturb the beet's consummate composure!

Now, to some people, peace of mind means beet-like imperturbability—the sublime tranquillity of a vegetable. They believe that inward peace is possible only as they develop the same hard-boiled indifference toward life's unpleasant experiences. No matter what life hurls at you, become completely unaware of it, they advise, giving it no chance to penetrate your armor. Excitability is gross! Studiously ignore the most peremptory demands which troubles can make. Only thus will you remain free from the sorrows and headaches of the world.

But the trouble with this technique is: it works successfully only for vegetables. Neither you nor I can possibly gain the imperturbability of a beet, simply because we are not beets or lumps of inert beings on which the universe exerts its incontestable power. We are human souls made in the spiritual image of

God, and we are responsible for determining the quality of our living, regardless of how it may be assailed from without. Although we are indeed human, lured by the tuggings of the flesh, you and I are also able to respond to the tuggings of the Divine. We do not find inward peace by letting go of the Divine and moving down through descending levels of creation till we become brothers and sisters of the beet. *Quietude of spirit, rather, is found as we move upward through ascending levels of creation in response to that Divine tugging.* We are not designed to deal with worries by learning only how to slam the door in their faces. We overcome anxiety not by pretending it out of existence but by action which eliminates the causes which produce it. With the power God lends us, we are to hew out within ourselves a condition of peace. So much for beet-like imperturbability!

Other persons attempt to escape from their anxieties and worries into *bovine placidity.* But have you ever stared for thirty seconds straight into the vacuous brown eyes of a ruminating Guernsey cow resting at peace in a lush pasture? Here is unassailable contentedness, which neither tension, pressure, nor anxiety can disturb. Yet human beings sometimes think, *How wonderful! That sort of unruffled serenity is just what I want!* To them peace of mind means the mindless tranquillity of the milk cow. Inward quietude is found, they believe, as they emulate that worthy creature and escape to an existence in which trouble and anxiety do not exist. To them, peace is gained by building so many ramparts about life that nothing can penetrate their defenses. Like a medieval baron in his castle, they can run water into the moat, pull up the drawbridge, lower the portcullis, and relax in the ultimate kind of security. Their "castle" is whatever in their minds passes for maximum security: an enlarging bank balance perhaps, or a safe job with a promotional future and mounting status, or a sound insurance and retirement program, or membership in the most respectable church or club, and the like.

But the problem with this approach to peace of mind is—it is designed for cattle, not for immortal souls. It is futile for you or me to renounce our duties and responsibilities in the hope of finding inward tranquillity. Sleeping Beauty had peace within her hedge of thorns, but she is a character of fiction. The day of the monastery as the best means of finding peace is gone. Exactly the opposite is the truth. *Authentic peace which flows out of fellowship with God is available to you and me at the very moment we are busiest dealing with practical affairs.* For peace comes as we rid ourselves of our troubles by eliminating the causes which create them. And this requires perseverance. The psalmist instructed: "Seek peace, and pursue it" (Ps. 34:14). God's peace comes to us not as we retreat into bovine placidity when the going gets rough, but rather as we advance under fire to bring all of our living under discipleship to Jesus.

Third, there are persons who seek inward peace by retreating into *idiotic blythness.* In Victorian drama, when the villain has abducted the daughter, the father puts hand to brow and, collapsing on the horsehair sofa, cries, "Let me not think . . . !" But this is an unhappy parable of some contemporary life. In crises which threaten to destroy their serenity and balance, many individuals collapse helplessly on some mental sofa and cry, "O, let me not think . . ." For our minds can be balky mules which do not like to be driven where they do not want to go. When unpleasant facts and discommoding situations appear, the mind instinctively tries to take refuge in unbelief—"This can't be happening to me!"—in protestation that everything is still all right. Here is an attitude which advises: "The only way to keep your spirit blythe is to conceal it from threatening distresses and tensions."

But should either you or I carry this philosophy to its logical conclusion, we would come to live in a dreamworld of our own devising. This leads to madness—literally—the disease of schizophrenia. Rather, we show mental maturity when we seek inward peace not by vigorously slamming our mind's doors on everything which is tormenting or troublesome. *We find peace of mind only as we wrestle with those torments and troubles till, in God's strength, we overcome them and they disappear.* "There will be glory and honor and peace," wrote Paul, "for everyone who leads a righteous and helpful life" (Rom. 2:10, VV).

I like to remember the philosophy of a domestic who said one day to her employer, "You know, Miz Bessie, sometimes trouble is so high you can't climb over it. Sometimes trouble is so wide you can't walk around it. Sometimes trouble is so deep you can't dig under it. So I figure the only way to beat trouble is to duck my head and wade right through!"

You and I grow in spirit as we deal vigorously with the causes which create the problems and anxieties which beset us.

We are not contending against flesh and blood, but against the principalities, against the powers, against the world rulers of this present darkness, against the spiritual hosts of wickedness in the heavenly places. Therefore take the whole armor of God, that you may be able to withstand in the evil day, and having done all, to stand (Eph. 6:12-13).

28.

Learn to Live One Day
at a Time

Give priority to God's Kingdom and his goodness, and everything you need will be provided. Therefore do not worry about tomorrow, for tomorrow will take care of itself. Today offers as many troubles as you can handle (Matt. 6:32-33, VV).

When Jesus said, "Do not be anxious about tomorrow," he was saying in effect, "Concentrate on living only one day at a time." To be sure, we are to have forethought for the future. Yet if you and I try to handle intelligently and devotionally more than one day at a time, anticipating in our thoughts and emotions the burdens of the days, weeks, and months ahead, we may become disorganized and panicky.

In our disorganization we do not deal effectively with those burdens, and in our panic we may either lessen our trust in God and fall back on our inadequate strength, or do exactly the opposite and drop everything with a thud onto God's lap and try to walk away. Each may bring disaster because neither is what God has planned. He expects us to deal with each individual day with all our resources and His. *So as you and I bring all our powers of self-reliance and trust in God to bear on the opportunities and problems which each day presents, we follow the laws of spiritual growth which closely parallel those of physical growth.*

Think about how a baby grows. When a mother goes to the supermarket, she does not buy in one order all the food which her infant will consume during the forthcoming year. And even if she could, when she gets home she does not

open all the cans of baby food which she did buy, warm
them in a mammoth kettle, stuff them into her infant, and
then exclaim, "Now, that's *that* for a week!" How convenient
it would be if a mother needed to feed her baby only every
other day. But babies are not made like that, and, thank
goodness, neither are adults! Our needs can be met only by
day-to-day meals.

Now, in like manner it becomes possible for you and me
to deal intelligently and victoriously with life because each
of our years divides into 365 manageable days. We gain
maximum benefit from life when we learn how to deal creatively with one day at a time, not worrying about the future.
And when we do this, at least three things can happen which
will make our everyday living pleasanter and more mean-
ingful—items which are among God's wise provision for our
needs.

First, our burdens become more manageable. It is related that a
slightly-built young man, being interviewed for the position
of lifeguard at a beach, was asked, "Suppose a three-hun-
dred-pound woman suddenly began thrashing about wildly
in deep water and needed to be brought ashore. What would
you do?"

The young man frowned and muttered, "Three-hundred
pounds!" Then his face lightened and he answered confidently, "I reckon I could make two trips!" It was a wrong
answer, of course, and he didn't land the job. But his was
a suggestive answer which might work quite well in other
situations. Wherever possible, by our breaking up into several parts a job or burden which would be too big for either
you or me, couldn't we reduce it to manageable size?

This is exactly what God intended for humankind to do
with life itself, when at creation there was established the
pattern of darkness and light, thereby ensuring the endless
succession of new days with fresh starts. For every burden
becomes lighter as it is divided. Of course, the personal

problems which plague us are not always little matters which can easily be made right. Sometimes they are major problems which, if dropped on us all at once, would far outweigh our resources and powers. But when we take Jesus' words seriously about not being anxious over tomorrow, we can begin to whittle down those burdens day by day. The three-hundred pounders we can make up into ten daily packages of thirty pounds each—easier burdens for us to handle.

Second when we live just day by day, our strength will prove to be sufficient for each day's demands. The Killdeer Mountains in North Dakota, like many other western buttes, are capped with a fifty-foot layer of rimrock which restricts easy ascent to a particular narrow defile through which the climber must wriggle. During the 1880s, a small band of Indians was attacked by a larger party of whites. The Indians fled up this ravine, and just beyond the narrow defile laid an ambush. As fast as a pursuer came through the defile he was picked off. The surviving whites wisely abandoned the pursuit and withdrew from the mountains.

Isn't this a parable of how you and I may make the most of the spiritual stamina we possess? When we find ourselves unable to deal effectively with a task or trial awaiting us, there are often approaches by which we may break up that problem into a division of days. We may pass it through the narrow defile of time, as it were, so it will reach us in units with which we can deal. We can succeed because we can hurl our full strength against the partial and divided strength of "the enemy."

Some years ago there was a tragic airline crash in Newfoundland which took the life of the discoverer of insulin, Sir Frederick Banting. The pilot of the stricken craft, Captain J. C. Mackey, has described how in spite of injuries he set out to crawl for help. Several times he nearly gave up and slumped in the brush in utter exhaustion. But he wrote:

Slowly my energy would come back and rouse me to make
one more try. I set myself little tasks. I set my goal as merely
the next rock, the next bush. When I made that, I fell down
and waited to see if my heart would come back. Then I
would set a new goal. The two miles traveled that afternoon
took me from noon to dusk.

But the captain made it because his strength was sufficient
for each little chunk of the problem which he accepted as his
present task. When you and I live "just for today," our
measure of strength will prove to be sufficient for our need.

*Third: our problems will sometimes of themselves diminish in size and
intensity as we deal with them at a day-to-day pace.* This means our
worrying about them at all has been wasted. How often
anticipated fears are proven to be little more than mirages
which, when we draw near, shimmer a moment and then
disappear. Now, of course, a certain percentage of our troubles are solid genuine facts which loom bigger and bigger the
closer we come to them. These actual trials and anxieties we
can handle through avenues already suggested. *But I have been
astonished at how many of my problems, which from a distance have
seemed to be insurmountable, suddenly become little more than mirages
when I attempt to take the first day's "bite" out of them.* On the
highway, steep hills often flatten out when I reach them, and
so do many of my worries which have loomed forbiddingly
ahead. And when you and I learn to live day by day, we will
eliminate the stress and strain we might have experienced
from these concerns and anxieties, but failed to do so because they either flattened out or disappeared.

God provides opportunity for us to mature spiritually by
breaking down all our living into a series of new days, each
offering a fresh beginning. "So we do not lose heart. Though
our outer nature is wasting away, our inner nature is being
renewed every day." (2 Cor. 4:16).

29.
Accept the Interrelatedness of Prayer and Action

A man is justified by works and not by faith alone. . . . For as the body apart from the spirit is dead, so faith apart from works is dead (Jas. 2:24-26).

Two little girls were coming home from Sunday School when a few drops of rain fell. In alarm one child cried, "Goodness, we ought to get down on our knees and pray to God that we won't get our Sunday dresses wet!"

But the other girl cried, "We'd better pray while we run."

This epitomizes the relationship which ought to exist, within our everyday living, between praying and acting. Some years ago our church's young people were studying the Book of Jonah before dramatizing it. As we worked through the story we came on several verses which clarified for me the responsibility for purposeful living which God expects me to shoulder. God had instructed the prophet Jonah to go to Nineveh, capital of enemy Assyria, and to challenge the people to repent of its many sins. But because Jonah would have rather seen the Assyrians destroyed, he headed for Spain by boat, hoping to go beyond the boundary of God's domain. The Scripture states, however, that . . .

the Lord hurled a great wind upon the sea, and there was a mighty tempest on the sea, so that the ship threatened to break up. Then the mariners were afraid, and each cried to his god; and they threw the wares that were in the ship into the sea, to lighten it for them (Jonah 1:4-5).

Notice that the account does not read, "The sailors were afraid, and each cried out to his god," and then stop there. Nor does it only declare that the "sailors were afraid, and threw things overboard to lighten the ship." In these variants there are significant omissions. *The mariners met this crisis with both a religious and an occupational response.* Their immediate thought was prayer, and they prayed. But note that the ship did not founder while they were on their knees! Because they realized that the Lord helps those who help themselves, they added to their prayers, deeds. They threw things overboard to increase the vessel's buoyancy.

Within our family's camping experience there is a knot which we used more frequently than any other, the double half-hitch. A single half-hitch is a good foundation for a variety of knots but has no use by itself. Add to it another single half-hitch, though, and a knot is tied which will not pull free.

Does this not express the relationship which should exist *between our practice of praying and our instinct of acting?* Prayer is basic, but if it is to yield the whole of its power, it must be blended with the habit of action. This is James's essential combination of faith with works. Thus it is a double half-hitch of deeds united with prayers which binds us to the onward movement of God's purposes. You and I, as the little girl suggested, are to pray while we run.

Yet I do not find this easy. Frequently I discover myself *acting without praying.* Here is but a single half-hitch which will be ineffectual till I unite it with the other half-hitch of prayer. Perhaps you have heard someone cry in a sudden emergency, "This is no time for prayer. Do something! Anything!" For them, prayer has its place in a leisurely, orderly world; the minute a crisis appears, prayer "clutters up" the situation. And further, in addition to believing that there are occasions when prayer is stupid, there are individuals who believe that there are areas of personal behavior which their devotion need never invade. How readily do you and I pray for wisdom in spending the family income? How often do we use prayer when crucial decisions must be made? How willing are we to use prayer, along with love, encouragement, and discipline, in our efforts to raise superior children? Perhaps it is impractical to "carry everything to God in prayer"; *yet is not the quintessence of praying our effort to live under the aspect of eternity?* And such living demands praying.

Sometimes, however, you and I may fall into the opposite habit—*that of praying without acting on our prayers.* Again, isn't this but a single half-hitch which lacks the completing half-hitch of action? It is dangerous to lean too heavily on God's responsibility and not enough on our own. "The little boy who fell in the mud puddle and prayed to God to lift him out, stayed there a good long time!"

In his book, *Tales of South Florida Pioneers,* Jack Beater told that when Captain Bill Collier's schooner was nearing Key West it ran into a fierce squall. He sent his three small boys and other passengers down into the cabin for safety. Shortly thereafter, the jibboom was carried away, and the *Speedwell* heeled over with decks awash. The jib topsail began splitting, and the deckhands were sent forward to clear away the damage. A "jackleg missionary preacher" had stayed on deck to help, and when it was apparent that shortly the vessel would turn turtle, Captain Collier made the only decision that would keep the vessel afloat. He thrust an axe into the preacher's hands and told him to run to the waist and cut the mainsheet which would bring the mainsail down immediately and put the ship back on even keel.

But instead of responding to the command, the preacher

dropped the axe and, falling to his knees, began fervently to pray. Within moments the ship overturned, and all within the cabin were drowned.

Now contrast this with an incident in Hartzell Spence's account of Francisco Orellano's discovery of the Amazon River. His record of that voyage from the headwaters down to the mouth is an endless story of starvation, treachery, snakes, crocodiles, disease, and Indian attack. It is related that when the brigantine was in danger of being swept toward certain destruction through a froth of white water and the crew was paralyzed with fright, the priest, Father Carvajal, plunged into the dangerous current with a line in his teeth, swam ashore, and secured the line to a tree, thus saving them all.

In commenting on this quick-thinking action by the "prayingest man" among them, Orellano said, "I believe that a man who prays when action is required is a fool, and God knows him for a fool. *God does not do for men what they should do for themselves! Had Father Carvajal prayed, instead of carrying a line ashore, he would have been drowned, and we with him!*"

Thus, we are to "Pray without ceasing" (1 Thess. 5:17, KJV), but never without acting!

Of course, there are times when you and I lift to God matters which lie entirely beyond our control. This is right, and we may leave such matters in His hands. But we frequently pray about situations which are at least partly within our control. Then there rests on us the obligation *to offer ourselves as instruments through whom God may bring that part of our prayers to pass!* We are to help Him answer them, living our prayers into reality.

A conversation with Ranger-Naturalist Maurice Sullivan has long been in my mind. We had climbed Mount Katahdin in Maine, and during the long descent in late afternoon he spoke about forest fires. The kind of blaze which should most be feared is the crown fire, which leaves the ground and on the wings of wind leaps through treetops faster than a deer can run. Ranger Sullivan then told of a ranger convocation where rookies were being introduced to the various kinds of fires. One of the newcomers asked the chief ranger a question which was in the minds of them all: "Sir, what shall we do if the fire crowns?"

The reply of the chief ranger was both prompt and pungent: "Pray for rain and run like——!" Exactly!

Dynamic, mature living is not maintained by prayer without action nor yet by action without prayer, but rather by God's strength and ours conjoined. With the little girl, pray that it stops raining, or with the sailors, pray for a calm? Yes, because these things are within God's province. Lighten the ship, pick ourselves out of the mud? Yes, because these are our responsibility.

Borden P. Bowne has summarized this guideline for creative living with these words: "Pray as though it all depends on God while acting as though it all depends on you!"

Someone may say, "You have faith and I have works." Show me your faith apart from your works, and I by my works will show you my faith (Jas. 2:18).

30.
Discover Your Need to Get Involved

Bear one another's burdens, and so fulfil the law of Christ. . . . Let us not grow weary in well-doing, for in due season we shall reap, if we do not lose heart. So then, as we have opportunity, let us do good to all men (Gal. 6:2,9-10).

When in sudden anger Moses killed an Egyptian overseer who was abusing a Hebrew slave, he fled to Midian where he became a shepherd. But as the lot of the slaves back in Egypt grew worse, the Lord commanded Moses, "Come, I will send you to Pharaoh so that you may rescue my people."

Moses, however, made the classic human reply, "Who, me? That's not my bag. I'm a wanted man in Egypt anyway. Pharaoh has a contract out on me, and the reward posters are still up in the marketplaces. I'd be putting my head on the chopping block."

God replied gently, "But I will go with you."

Apparently, this was an insufficient guarantee. Moses persisted, "It's a dangerous thing to incite mutiny among the slaves, as I did. What if Pharaoh says to me, 'Just who is this God of yours, that He can protect you from my anger?' What then?"

God answered, "Tell Pharaoh that I am the God of Abraham, Isaac, and Jacob."

But still Moses did not want to swap his present comfort for unknown perils. "Pharaoh will say, 'Who are those peo-

ple? I never heard of them. Now prove that you do indeed
have a commission from this God!"

God acknowledged Moses' point. To provide the necessary credentials, God showed Moses that when he threw his
staff to the ground, it would become a cobra—which should
be proof enough for any doubter. Stubbornly, Moses fought
off becoming involved in any quixotic rescue attempt.
"Lord," he burst out, "Can't You send somebody else?"

The record shows, then, that the Lord's anger was kindled
against Moses. "You will go!" He stated with finality. "Now
get with it!" And Moses went.

Essentially, Moses was asking a major question: "Just why
should I get mixed up in other people's concerns?" He had
done it once back in Egypt and was forced to run for his life.
"It just leads to trouble all around!" And this attitude is
present today in the modern cult of noninvolvement. There
is even a blank bumper sticker "for those who don't want
to get involved!"

Dag Hammarskjöld, former secretary general of the United Nations till his tragic death in Africa, left a devotional
diary called *Markings* which he labeled as "a sort of White
Book concerning my negotiations with myself and with
God." In 1935 Hammarskjöld, entered these words: "In our
era, the road to holiness necessarily passes through the
world of action." That is, no longer may you or I enjoy a
delicious sense of piety derived from our own carefully-
nurtured thoughts and attitudes, without being accountable
also for acting on behalf of our fellows. *We must be as socially
holy as we are religiously holy!* There can be no such creature as
a socially-noninvolved Christian. This is a complete contra-
diction in terms which I have expressed:

The Incarnation of God in Christ Jesus
    Outcrops not in just theological veins,

But also appears in concerns for diseases
And hunger and rodents and foul-smelling drains!

Therefore, the path which you and I must tread necessarily leads through private devotion into public concern that the kingdom of God may draw closer each day. The willingness to seek holines through creative relations with those in need separates the authentic Christian from the pious fraud.

There are practical answers to Moses' question and ours: "Why should I get involved with other people's troubles?" such as that it offers unexpected satisfactions, and even sometimes makes a dent in social problems. But for you and me there is a more basic reason, namely that this is the way Jesus lived. If we are to be faithful to His Way, we must walk in it! It is that simple, and that difficult! Paul wrote similarly to the church people in Philippi: "Let your bearing towards one another arise out of your life in Christ Jesus" (Phil. 2:5, NEB). Here is the reason for the servanthood of the practicing Christian today. For if we have been sensitized by our discipleship, we recognize that we must be where God's action is.

It is unfortunate that within Christendom there are individuals who sincerely believe that they are not called to serve their fellows' needs. The epitaph of one of them reads, "He slid away from everything unpleasant." It was said of a certain renowned clergyman, "Whenever they met for counsel, John was present; whenever they met for work, John was absent." This is reminiscent of the deacon who prayed fervently, "Use me, Lord, O use me—in a strictly advisory capacity!" What tragedies! For life is full of Jericho roads along which the lost, the lonely, and the wounded cry for help. You and I travel those same roads.

In our finer moments we sense that we cannot take refuge in such excuses as Moses offered, "I'm not the right person;

nobody will listen to me; it will cost me my job; it's highly
dangerous; I wouldn't have the faintest idea how to go about
it!" We honor the memory of Elizabeth Fry because she
refused to let someone else worry about England's prisons.
She knew that talking about servanthood was not enough. The road to
holiness does indeed necessarily pass through the world of
action. Growth in Christlike character is the result of our
acting as servants, not as masters. Like Jesus, we are not to
be ministered to but to minister. "We are ambassadors for
Christ, God making his appeal through us" (2 Cor. 5:20).

All may be summarized in an incident which August
Derleth related about the newly-founded village of Stough-
ton, Wisconsin, about 1840. One Saturday night when a
number of farm wives were waiting patiently in wagons
outside a saloon, a brawl broke out inside. Because of the
brutal reputation of some of the participants, no one dared
to enter the place to stop it. Finally, a farmer and his wife,
who had come to town for supplies and were passing by,
learned what was going on. The husband said, "Emmy, I'm
going in."

"But it isn't your fight," she said sharply.

"This is our town," he replied, "and saloon fights are bad.
Someone might get killed."

"But why should you be the one to go?" she wailed.

He replied gently, "Those men inside are our neighbors."
Disengaging her hand, he jumped from the wagon and entered the saloon just as a window burst under the impact of
a chair.

To the amazement and relief of the anxious watchers, the
clamor and racket began to die away, till everything was
still. Then the peacemaker came out. "They're done, now,"
he announced. "You women can collect your men."

"Because they are our neighbors!" This is ultimately why Moses
went back to Egypt in spite of danger to his life? This is why

Jesus told the story of the Good Samaritan, in which every individual in need is our neighbor. This is the reason that whenever we respond personally to some human problem, we act out the servanthood of Jesus!

Thus as we discover and act on our need to become personally involved with others, we move toward greater spiritual maturity—particularly when we act out of holy indignation.

> If anyone has the world's goods and sees his brother in need, yet closes his heart against him, how does God's love abide in him? Little children, let us not love in word or speech but in deed and truth (1 John 3:17-18).

31.
Learn the Necessity of Holy Indignation

Rejoice with those who rejoice, weep with those who weep (Rom. 12:15).

In studying the records of Jesus' life, I have learned that our Master was essentially a joyous person, and that Christianity ought to be revealed as the most joyous religion on earth. Jesus knew moments of unhappiness and sorrow, but the totality of His life, His message, and resurrection celebrates the good news that "God with men is now residing." And yet, because Jesus wanted everyone, even the humblest peasant, to know the joy He possessed, He frequently gave vent to righteous wrath against those persons or conditions which kept individuals from attaining that joy. Jesus was capable of holy indignation—anger free from sin—and thereby legitimized my need today for the expression of a parallel righteous wrath. "Justified anger," exclaimed a philosopher, "is one of the sinews of the soul; he who lacks it has a maimed mind."

In a letter to the Christians in Ephesus, Paul wrote a sentence which at first may seem self-contradictory. He urged them, "Be ye angry, and sin not" (4:26, KJV). This sounds like telling children that they may play in the mud if they will not get dirty. But holy indignation played a creative role in Jesus' life, so it should also have a creative function in your life and mine.

Mark 3 relates how one sabbath Jesus found a man with
a withered hand. Because strict laws proscribed healings on
that day, everyone watched this renowned healer with cov-
ert intensity. If Jesus cured the cripple, the Pharisees could
bring heavy charges against Him. Jesus was perfectly aware
of the situation and became incensed. Calling the cripple to
Him He asked those who watched, "Are we allowed to do
good on the sabbath, or to do evil? to save a life or to destroy
one?" But everyone remained silent. Then Jesus loosed the
bonds of His indignation. The record states, "He looked
around at them with anger, grieved at their hardness of
heart, and said to the man, 'Stretch out your hand.' He
stretched it out, and his hand was restored" (3:5).

Jesus blazed with indignation *because He was mightily concerned
with human values. When those values were denied, He could not help
but burst into righteous wrath.* He would not be worthy of our
loyalty had He not! Whenever He encountered situations
which were aimed at narrowing down individuals' lives, He
set Himself in forceful opposition. In this incident, as in
numerous others, Jesus became a one-man social action
committee, using the power of faith to free people from the
deadening hand of religious traditionalism.

Might it not be, then, that you and I are poor followers
of Jesus till we become indignant over human injustice?
Even within the church there are those who say, "What
happens to other people is between them and God. I have
no commission to interfere. It's our job to stick to the gospel." But every church which aims to engage in authentic
service for its Lord must learn to feel holy indignation and
act on it. How essential for us to acquire the sensitivity of
Jesus to human misery and let righteous anger guide us into
activities of social concern which will help to bring all of
society under the mind of Christ.

But this is only the first half of Paul's injunction. There

follow four words of a distinctly qualifying character. "Be angry"—yes—"but do not sin"! This is not an easy combination of commands. How shall I determine when it is right to be angry? In what direction, and for how long? The blind hymn-writer, George Matheson, once ruefully confessed, "There are times when I do well to be angry, but I have often mistaken the times." How can I be moved by anger and yet not commit stupid or unthinking acts which I shall later regret? How can I be sure that my anger is *holy indignation?*

Well, there is an answer in the Gospels. *It is that Jesus' anger came not out of a resentment or hate He held toward troublesome persons, but out of a great love He held for all people.* The condition of resentment is dangerously negative, but outflowing concern is creatively positive. If Jesus had not cared deeply about what happened to individuals, He would not have been concerned about their mistreatment. His anger was one natural aspect of His total relation to people. Because He cared about the least and humblest of persons, He rejoiced when happiness came their way; He comforted them when sorrows gripped them, and He burned with righteous indignation when they were cheated, exploited, or denied their rights as immortal souls. *Only anger born of love is holy.*

Here is how to test whether the anger I sometimes feel is holy: *Does that anger arise on behalf of my fellow persons because of my affection and concern for them?* Or does it simply emerge as a response to certain abrasive ways in which *I myself have been treated?* If anger boils up in me because someone is making trouble for me, that anger may be a natural emotion, but it is not a holy one. Wrath becomes righteous when it springs out of my positive, outgoing concern for other persons who are being abused.

This is demonstrated time and again in Jesus' life. His was a totally unselfish anger, loosed only on behalf of others. He never permitted Himself to become angry over what His enemies did to Him personally. His last week on earth could have been crowded with anger at how people were treating Him. He was arrested secretly at night, chained, and hauled off to prison, in Soviet style under cover of darkness, where He was interrogated and mocked, beaten and spat upon, and hung up by nailed hands and feet to die, then finally His side was pierced with a spear. Yet as the writer of 1 Peter declared, "When he was reviled, he did not revile in return; when he suffered, he did not threaten" (2:23). As the black spiritual puts it, "He never said a mumblin' word." Only when injustice was inflicted on another person did He give way to anger—a holy indignation.

By unhappy contrast, my anger often is a response to personal affronts. It comes as a result of someone setting himself against my will, thwarting my desires, making sport of my values, defying my influence. My cherished self has been attacked, and anger rises as an instantaneous response. This is not holy wrath, even though I may feel quite justified in giving vent to it; but, rather, *it is the kind most certainly causing me to sin, and, therefore, the kind which I speedily must bring under control!* The only responses I dare make to any form of anger I feel toward anyone, are the ones which Jesus demonstrated: patient forgiveness, depth of understanding, invincible affection, and the boundless willing of good.

Some years ago Bishop Bernard Shiel of Chicago attended a particular mass meeting called by a hate group to stir up race prejudice and religious intolerance. Finally, driven to righteous wrath by the speeches being made, the bishop made his way to the platform and for fifteen minutes denounced anti-Semitism, white supremacy, and other vile concepts which had been bellowed that night. The audience listened with growing hostility. His speech ended, the bishop began to leave the hall by the central aisle.

Suddenly, the silence was broken when a fanatical woman

blocked his path and screamed, "I'm a good Catholic, but you, you're only a nigger-lover, a Jew-lover. A Bishop! Ha! I say Rabbi Shiel!" Then she deliberately cleared her throat and spat on one side of the bishop's face. The woman was angry, and she sinned.

The mad roar which gradually had begun to rise suddenly died away. For the bishop, with all the quiet dignity of his office, had turned the other cheek and stood there, waiting.

The woman stood immovable as did the hundreds about her. Then, as though a sudden chill had gripped her, she began to shake violently. With a gasp, she turned and fled.

In the utter silence which followed, Bishop Shiel spoke only eight words: "Rabbi? That is what they called our Lord." And as he left the hall, many others straggled out shamefacedly. The meeting was over. The Bishop had been angry—*but had not sinned.*

Yes, you and I must know how to get angry—in other persons' defense. We are to act courageously in their behalf, using what Gandhi called "soul force." For as we learn the necessity of expressing holy indignation—and only the holy kind—we will help to untangle the knotted strands of personal relationships. And in doing so, we will grow in favor both with God and others.

> If you are angry, do not let your anger lead you into sin; do not let sunset find you still nursing it; leave no loop-hole for the devil (Eph. 4:26-27, NEB).

32.
Accept the Inevitability of Suffering

Keep your conscience clear, so that, when you are abused, those who revile your good behavior in Christ may be put to shame. For it is better to suffer for doing right, than for doing wrong (1 Pet. 3:16-17).

Years ago in a Denver hospital an unknown patient wrote on the wall near the bed a poem, the first stanza of which began: The cry of man's anguish went up to God, "Lord, take away pain," and concluded: "Lord, take away pain from the world thou hast made, That it love thee the more."

More than once I have offered this prayer, for it is a universal cry. No more could Shylock have his pound of flesh without any blood than could you or I have life without suffering. The inescapability of bearing pain, and the use to which Jesus put it on the cross, lie at the heart of our faith and demand that we deal with it creatively. "It has been granted to you," wrote Paul, "that for the sake of Christ you should not only believe in him but also suffer for his sake" (Phil. 1:29).

Through the eyes of Jesus, we see that the universe is friendly, that God's world is wholesome, good, and an expression of His vast love for us. But now and again, moments of pain—experiences of physical or mental suffering, or persecution from our fellows—make us question these beliefs. If God loves us, why does He allow hundreds of kinds of accidents to occur? Why does He permit loved ones to go astray, bringing pain both to themselves and their families? Why doesn't He silence those who ridicule our Christian stance? Why doesn't He prevent nations from invading territories which do not belong to them, plunging peoples into misery, and pushing the world a step nearer to global catastrophe? Wouldn't we have better reason to love God were He to take from us the curse of suffering?

But to all such questions God has remained silent—just as when His own Son was slain. The earth's multibillion prayers for the ending of suffering and anxiety have reached His throne, so are we to conclude that He is deliberately choosing to ignore our continuing pleas? Perhaps some searching questions should be asked.

What would happen if God suddenly were to pass a miracle and entirely eliminate suffering and pain from our earth? We would look around and see disease conquered, accidents ended, the mass murder we call war vanquished, civil rights for everyone attained, mental anguish for our own misdeeds or those of our friends terminated, and friendly acceptance of our words and deeds from those who disagree with us. Wouldn't we think that the kingdom of God had appeared, bringing us into full harmony with God and our neighbors?

This sounds almost too good to be true—and very likely it is. For I am set in this world to grow a soul, and I must work at it with earthly tools. I must use life's varied materials to develop a personality and a character which will be useful in a spiritual realm after death. Through the experiences and relationships afforded by my family and friends, my employment and my church, my schools and recreation, I can create that personality and character by taking the common materials of everyday living and shaping them for eternity.

Now, *one of the most valuable of these earthly materials which I must use is suffering of every kind—physical, mental, and spiritual—whether on my own behalf or on behalf of others.* From my bitter experiences may issue a veritable bouquet of benefits such as ruggedness of soul, tenacity of intention, capacity for compassion, the willingness to sacrifice, and above all, a fresh insight into the meaning of joyous, inconquerable love. Without such traits as these, I am nothing! Of course, there is far too much needless suffering and pain within life, and I must be involved with holy indignation to eliminate it. Even so, enough will remain to provide material for spiritual growth!

Suppose that when Arthur Rubinstein was young he detested certain aspects of his piano lessons, and his teacher said, "All right, Arthur, we will study harmony, notation, sight-reading, and dynamics, but we will let the finger exercises go." Had that been true, Rubinstein might have become a good pianist but never a great one. In like manner, if I want to gain the ability "to withstand in the evil day," must I not practice the "finger exercises of the soul"! *And one exercise which perhaps most completely underlies all Christlike growth is the ability to utilize creatively the rough places in my life.* Paul often demonstrated this ability; he wrote: "For the sake of Christ, then, I am content with weaknesses, insults, hardships, persecutions, and calamities; for when I am weak, then am I strong" (2 Cor. 12:9-10). The suffering poet in Denver recognized this paradox:

> Then answered the Lord to the cry of his world,
> "Shall I take away pain,
> And with it the power of the soul to endure,
> Made strong by the strain?"

For if God were to eliminate suffering, would not that endanger the splendid ruggedness of soul which you and I may obtain?

And we must also ask, "Can God remove suffering without also removing the kindred character traits, such as pity,

sympathy, and self-sacrifice, which are shaped in the searing
flames of our own suffering?" The head nurse of a hospital
once told me that a woman rarely becomes the best of nurses
till she herself has "cried out of the depths." From those
experiences, then, come a fund of pity and an overflowing
compassion for her patients who are learning in such pain
what she learned. From her loving recollection of the devotion others gave to her care, she will find a similar capacity
for self-forgetful service. From her realization of how those
who loved her suffered in spirit with her, she will come to
possess a parallel gift of empathy. Through her suffering she
will find invaluable spiritual capital.

Just as my soul has its "finger exercises" which help it to
become rugged, so it has its disciplines which are fused into
my life by pain and suffering. *Were God to pass a miracle so that
all suffering and pain were removed, along with them would go those
restraining disciplines which hold my life true to its eternal goals.* My
efforts to create a nobler personality and a better world
would collapse in failure. The hospitalized poet, therefore,
made God continue His answer to mankind's plea:

> "Shall I take away pity that knits heart to heart,
>   And sacrifice high?
> Will ye lose all your heroes who lift from the fire
>   White brows to the sky?"

For God to eliminate suffering would wipe out the interior
virtues and disciplines which you and I need in our quest for
larger souls.

And finally, you and I must ask, "Might not ridding the
world of suffering also rid it of love?" The kind of soul we
have depends on the kind of love we have. The finest love
is what we have found through suffering and can therefore
offer to other sufferers. Our pain may be in body or in soul;

it may be our own or pain we share with another person, but it can produce the love which ennobles our living. And by the same token, should God take away pain, the figure of a Man on a Cross would also become meaningless —a figure which now stands for the redeeming love of God. "Although he was a Son," declares Hebrews, "he learned obedience by what he suffered; and being made perfect he became the source of eternal salvation to all who obey him" (Heb. 5:8-9). Suppose that Jesus had fled from the cross and escaped into Egypt? Would He today be our Savior? In this poem, the Almighty concludes with these words:

"Shall I take away love that redeems with a price
    And smiles at its loss?
Can ye spare from your lives that would climb unto mine
    The Christ on His cross?"

For you and me, therefore, to face boldly and use creatively whatever suffering and pain become our lot is to "ride the winds that lift the highest."

After you have suffered a little while, the God of all grace, who has called you to his eternal glory in Christ, will himself restore, establish, and strengthen you (1 Pet. 5:10).

33.
Live as Though Divine Healing Is Likely

"But that you may know that the Son of man has authority on earth to forgive sins"—he said to the paralytic—"I say to you, rise, take your pallet and go home." And he rose, immediately took up the pallet and went out before them all; so that they were amazed and glorified God, saying, "We never saw anything like this!" (Mark 2:10-12).

A woman once commented to me, "I've just been watching a television program about divine healing. Nothing that I saw really persuaded me that it could happen. Do you believe in it?"

At that time I had had no personal experience which pointed toward a divine healing. But I replied, "This whole subject is shrouded in mystery which both honest adventurers and charlatans have sought to penetrate. But I find it helpful to live in the expectation that divine healing may occur when I need it." And now that I believe I have participated in such healing, I commend this attitude to you.

In dealing rationally rather than emotionally or gullibly with this matter, we need to recognize four inherent difficulties.

(1) *The first is: it is not easy to agree on a definition of divine healing.* Is it a cure which takes place utterly without human agency? Does it occur without the help of doctors and nurses, hospitals and medicines, and the encouragement of loved ones? Does it happen in spite of the patient's own unbelieving attitude? Does divine healing permit the assistance of clergymen and spiritually-gifted laypeople or the prayers of distraught family members? Or is God's power the only

factor? Or would it be interpreted wholly as a miracle, an upsetting of natural laws or the intrusion of the supernatural in violation of known laws? Or is divine healing simply a response of the body to laws which are not yet identified? Does the Holy Spirit act directly within a human body to effect a cure through His own power alone?

(2) *In a real sense, all healing is divine anyway!* God has built into the human body the capacity for self-healing. Therefore, is it not logical that, utilizing this very healing process God has placed within us, He could speed up or increase the healing-rate so it takes not a month but a minute? And if all healing has a divine aspect, how can I say, "This particular cure of mine or my wife's or my friend's was actually intrusively divine in origin?"

(3) *It may be difficult to recognize a genuine bit of divine healing when it does take place.* It may happen more frequently than you or I may think. We are aware of our dependence on the medical profession, and do not wish to shortchange their helpfulness when they work on us for some illness. We are also aware of the psychosomatic tie-up between the health of our bodies and the vigor of our minds and spirits, and realize that we ourselves can make important contributions to our own cures.

(4) *Divine healing is muddied by the fact that it provides magnificent and dramatic opportunities for pure fraud!* There is proportionately as much racketeering in mere religion as in any other area of life! Under the cloak of religion, unscrupulous individuals have "taken" many simple-faithed individuals. It is good showmanship and highly profitable to the showman. How can you and I distinguish the fraudulent from the genuine?

With these difficulties in mind, let me state what I have come to believe.

(a) *My body has a natural healing ability which automatically oper-*

ates on my behalf. Over the years it has fulfilled its functions well.

(b) I must follow the rules of good health which means that I must live as God intends me to. I cannot ignore or deliberately violate these "laws" and then hope to be made well by divine healing. That is, I may not live carelessly, let alone riotously, and then expect God to step in and miraculously repair the damage I have done to myself.

(c) There are times when authentic divine healing does take place. I have attended healing sessions sponsored by such world leaders as Brother Mandus and Dr. Robert Cochrane, and while such sessions resulted in no obvious or dramatic healings, I accept their testimony as true. Further, I believe that both my wife and myself have received healing which can be credited primarily to no other cause than the direct action of God. We now live, therefore, in the expectation that divine healing can occur when God grants it and when we need it.

But there are at least three conditions to be fulfilled. There are usually three parties involved in authentic spiritual healing. First, there is God Who has established the conditions under which such healing can occur, and Who stands ready to act.

Second, there is the sufferer, who must want to be cured, who must have confidence in God's power, and look to Him in expectancy that healing will result. But in addition, *the sufferer must be attempting to live in harmony with God's purposes and the laws of sound health, so that in the heart there is no obstacle blocking the inflow of God's power.*

Third, there is frequently, although not necessarily, a "healing agent" or "precipitator" who through his or her intercessory prayers and ministrations is able to effect a relation between the sufferer and God which the sufferer cannot make alone. Like forceps to a dentist or a scalpel to a surgeon, this mediator is an instrument of the healing process. He or she, too, must be in line with God's purposes, so that healing power may flow unobstructedly through them.

At those times when I have sought to be a healing agent, my tools have been prayer, a quiet infusion of confidence and holiness into the sufferer, and the physical "laying on of hands" along with this sort of prayer: "If Thou dost wish, Father, let Thy healing power flow through these hands and into this suffering child of Thine. Where there are forces of destruction at work, do Thou put them to rout. Where there are seeds of death sprouting, do Thou replace them with life-giving powers. May this person live, if it be Thy will, to love and serve Thee for the normal span of life till, in the fulness of maturity and with work accomplished, Thou dost receive this soul to Thyself with these words, 'Well done, good and faithful servant: enter Thou into the joy of thy Lord.' "

As I recall times when I have been such a mediator, I have been able to identify to my own satisfaction only two authentic cases of divine healing which flowed through my hands. I kept no record of my "batting average." Many sufferers have gotten well following my ministrations, some after long, hard fights; others have died. Yet divine healing may have occurred oftener. *Therefore as you and I meet the conditions, we have every right to look to God for divine healing.* And this attitude will make a difference in our day-to-day living.

> Is any among you suffering? Let him pray. . . . Is any among you sick? Let him call for the elders of the church, and let them pray over him, anointing him with oil in the name of the Lord; and the prayer of faith will save the sick man, and the Lord will raise him up (Jas. 5:13-15).

34.
Cast the Dark Bogey Out of Dying

We would not have you ignorant, brethren, concerning those who are asleep, that you may not grieve as others do who have no hope. For since we believe that Jesus died and rose again, even so, through Jesus, God will bring those who have fallen asleep (1 Thess. 4:13-14).

I have often heard that a person's faith is revealed by the confident manner in which he faces life. The opposite also may be true—that I have a trustworthy index to people's faith when I see them face death confidently.

Frank Crowninshield paid a particularly fine tribute to his brother Edward at his brother's death: "Although dying, he could brighten up a room!" To such a valiant soul, the Grim Reaper is neither grim nor a reaper; death is but the loving, indrawing action of the Almighty. Where did this figure of speech—the Grim Reaper—come from, anyway? It certainly is not a Christian concept. When death occurs at its proper place at the close of a useful life, *a more accurate metaphor might be that of the Joyous Sower, wherein the seed of an individual's life, dying to itself within the furrow of the grave, yields to the quickening impulse of God's warm Spirit and grows to an undreamed-of maturity in God's nearer presence.* When you and I attain the conviction that death need not be the final accounting of these often miss-pent years, but can be the springtime sowing of eternal life, we then cast the dark bogey out of dying. Death then becomes for us a symbol of promise and hope. We will sing with Whittier:

I know not where His islands lift
Their fronded palms in air;
I only know I cannot drift
Beyond His love and care.

But suppose someone were to ask you, "Are you afraid to die—say, this afternoon?" What might be your answer? Would the bogey jump out at you, or would you be "sustained and soothed by an unfaltering trust?" I cannot read your mind and heart to know what you might answer, but I can only read my own and report what I find there. In terms of family, of life work, and of personality growth, I find the answer to be both yes and no. First, the *yes* answers to: "Am I afraid to die this afternoon?"

(1) I would be immediately concerned about my *family responsibilities.* I cannot properly be freed from them till I have properly fulfilled them. The network of affections and duties I have purposefully developed within my family would be rudely fractured by my death, and I am not ready to see this happen. It is God's plan that a child shall grow into fullness of character and richness of personality within the framework of a religiously-oriented home. This we have sought for our four, and now they are in homes of their own. Thus my major responsibility for them is at an end, so my death this afternoon would sadden them but not threaten them. But then there are the grandchildren.

But it is also the intention of God that a husband and wife shall travel the long road together to its distant end. Like vines which have separate roots, but in growing entwine their branches into an indivisible unity, the couple increasingly intermingle their interests and accomplishments, their disappointments and dreams. Should death uproot one of our mingled vines, the forcible disentanglement of the interlacing tendrils of comradeship and affection would deal a severe blow to the survivor's whole being. Knowing this, I must confess that for my wife's sake, I am afraid to die now.

(2) But there is a second reason: *there remains work for me to do which is part of a network of economic, social, and religious responsibilities beyond the home.* For more than forty years I have offered leadership within Christian churches, and I continue that work now in retirement as I am able. I have sought to follow an inward vision of what task my current church and I should be accomplishing—a particular pattern of growth, usefulness, and service—and there are still parts of the task undone. I do not want to be interrupted at this point by death!

(3) The third reason why I would be worried over the prospect of dying shortly is one mentioned in the thirty-second guideline: *I believe that God has put me here into the world to grow a soul.* All else is secondary to this purpose. He has established me in a framework so vast and complex that I have a thousand different opportunities to enrich my spiritual life. But because God does not want me to be a wooden-headed dummy who speaks only when spoken through by divine ventriloquism—essentially God carrying on a dialogue with Himself!—He gives me the power to reject His purposes and substitute my own.

Now, I have abused this freedom at times and have not grown the soul yet that I should have. My fear of dying this afternoon is intensely personal, being rooted in the uncomfortable conviction that I am not ready to enter God's nearer presence. *I am not prepared at this moment to render an account of my stewardship.* Therefore, being unwilling to relinquish my role as a husband and father, being unready to consider my life work as finished, and acknowledging the scrawniness of the soul I ought to have been preparing for eternity, I confess frankly, "Yes, I would be afraid to die this afternoon."

But now the *no* answers must be given. Having shared

three *yes* reasons with you, I am constrained to deny them all and say firmly, "No, I am not afraid to die this afternoon." My conviction comes from faith, scriptural assurance, and experience.

(*a*) Take first the matter of *family responsibility*. Think of some family in your neighborhood whose husband and father has died. Don't you remember with warm approval the courage with which the bereaved wife, rising triumphantly over grief, continually schemed how to fill the new emptiness both in her life and that of her children? My children, as yours, have that kind of person as a parent. I can trust my wife to fulfill to the limits of her strength the parental responsibilities I might leave behind and to find creative ways to ease the desolate sense of loss. And because death in a neighborhood often releases a hidden kindliness in people which overflows in thoughtful needs, I expect that persons would seek out my wife in the hope of mitigating her shattering loneliness or of turning some sharp edge of insecurity. Yet over all, isn't it God who implants in hearts numbed with sorrow the power to move forward bravely? Isn't He the One Who gives the deepest comfort which consoles, and the guidance which heartens, wiping away the tears from our eyes? Were this not so, then death were more powerful than God. I am impelled to state, "No, for my family's sake I am not afraid to die."

(*b*) And what is true about my family is also true about *my life work*. I am confident that if you and I are doing God's will in our daily work, the responsibilities we have undertaken will one day be fulfilled whether we live or die. Paul told the Christians in Philippi that he was confident that God, who had begun a good work in them, would bring it to completion. I know that God will see that my unfinished work bears fruit, because He has a larger stake in it than I have! So although I am full of plans and dreams for what I want yet to accomplish before God calls me away, I can say confidently, "No, I am not afraid to die this afternoon."

(c) Now what about those *distressing times when I imagine myself before God's judgment bar,* documenting my unworthiness to enter His presence? Well, even as I bow in shame, a voice within me cries, "Hold on! God is not a hanging Judge. He does not deal with me according to my sins, nor punish me according to my iniquities. He knows what I am made of, remembering that it is dust!" And Paul added to the psalmist's (103:14) testimony to God's mercy: "God shows his love for us in that while we were yet sinners Christ died for us" (Rom. 5:8). *The Almighty has so great a fatherly concern for me that my very weaknesses bring forth His forgiveness and enlist His aid!*

I know that when death claims me, soon or late, I shall be convicted of wasting much of the substance of eternity in second-rate living and of failing to grow to my fullest potential. Yet I affirm that God gently will receive me into His eternal presence—all because of His loving grace.

A milestone in my spiritual growth is being able to cast the dark bogey out of dying.

> For we know that if the earthly tent we live in is destroyed, we have a building from God, a house not made with hands, eternal in the heavens (2 Cor. 5:1).

35.
Count on Life After Death

Do not become faint-hearted. Trust in God and have faith in me. My Father's house has many apartments—would I be saying this if it were not so?—and I am going to get one ready for each of you" (John 14:1-2, VV).

A man once philosophized to me, "When my death comes, that's the end of me as a personality. The whole of me is kaput. In the punctuation of my existence, the grave is not a semicolon but a final period. The tomb is not even a question mark but a concluding exclamation point!" Polished English—but mistaken! Others have suggested that the only immortality on which they can count is to be found in their children, in the institutions in which they have worked, or in the influence their memory may continue to exert on others. I hope for these sorts of immortality, but my expectation goes a great deal further.

In the quest for a Christian understanding of life, a basic question to answer is: "What is God's long-range purpose for us? For what reasons has He set us in this world with all its joys and sorrows, dangers and opportunities?" Earlier I said that God's purpose is to grow eternal souls. Now, let's explore this more fully, beginning with a simple illustration.

Just as there are certain farmers who exclusively produce milk, others who raise nothing but Aberdeen-Angus beef, and still others who choose truck gardening, so also God is a specialist in His own "agricultural" pursuits. *He is a character farmer.* The whole earth is His acreage, and we human beings

187

are His plantings. The crops which we produce are qualities of Christlike character. Because God is Spirit, the crops He most desires to harvest are those He can use for His holy purposes. Therefore, He is particularly concerned about our spiritual growth. Our personalities are His crops.

It is obvious God exerts far more care at safeguarding His plantings than any farmer does. Before the first frost the truck gardener picks all his tomatoes and puts them in his barn for processing. The vines he leaves because their work is done. The frost nips them, and they blacken and die. Later on the farmer may rake them into a heap and burn them or perhaps plow them back into the soil. At any rate, the vines vanish with the frost, and the harvested tomatoes are boxed for shipment to market.

What would you think of a farmer who, just before the harvest, takes his tractor and plows under his whole tomato crop? When I was living in Maine the Air Force was so anxious to build its great air base at Presque Isle that it bought several thousand acres of potato land ready to be harvested, and covered it with runways without allowing a single potato to be dug! Human beings sometimes do this with their crops. *But God never does that with His!* The frost of death kills the "vines," and our bodies go into the grave, but the fruits of our personality—that which is truly Christlike within us—survive within the Father's barns, to be used in whatever eternal enterprise He may choose.

By believing thus in the survival of my personality, my soul, I am not "indulging my ego," for this conviction is based on the highest idea we hold about God. We know that He is even more loving than our own parents, and our souls are infinitely more precious to Him than they are to our parents. Humankind has always had premonitions of God's intention to preserve what is immortal within us. Words-worth spoke of such feelings as "Intimations of Immortality." We have learned to cherish Christlike qualities because, in addition to their gracious enrichment of our living here on earth, *we sense that their fullest use lies in the realm of the Spirit beyond the grave.* God's purpose is to produce Christlike souls for service in His eternal Kingdom, and every holy instinct within me shouts that it is true.

From this conviction about personality survival after death, then, I am led inescapably to a second affirmation, namely, that *my personality and its component elements of character are intimately a part of my individuality.* What I mean by "individuality" are those qualities which make me peculiarly myself—"me-ness" as distinct from anyone else in the world. This quality of individuality also contains my personal value. For the best ideals we cherish put the highest price on individual worth. The best political system, democracy, the most advanced educational ideals, the most productive economic practice, and Christianity itself all underscore the primal value of individuality. *The kind of person God wants most is not stamped out in carload lots.* For God, each soul must be handwrought, bearing the distinguishing marks of its Shaper. He has given me the power to produce "me-ness," a totality of personality and character different from that of any other human being. As I attempt to live faithfully in Jesus' spirit, hammering out my life on the anvil of His example and companionship, I shape a personality all my own. It is by this individuality that I am known and recognized today, equally as by physical appearance. My spirit becomes as distinctive as my body, and as quickly identifiable.

Therefore I must inevitably conclude that *this individuality of mine, precious to God, will be perpetuated in eternity.* For if my Christlike qualities are to survive death, how can they be separated from my individuality? My "me-ness" cannot be centrifuged from my personality. God does not take the latter without the former. When I die, therefore, the Christ-like part of my total individuality, containing the "crop" of eternal qualities I have "grown," passes over intact into eternity. *I will be as identifiable there as I ever was here. And I will be able to recognize my loved ones who have gone on before.* The short-cuts to identification formerly provided by physical, bodily characteristics will, of course, be gone; but I will be able to distinguish my family and friends by the individuality of the Christlike spirits which they shaped while here on earth.

This means that the greater the amount of Christlike spirit to pass beyond the tomb, the easier will be the identification! The personality most richly bearing the marks of Christ in this life will be the most immediately recognizable in the next. *Shakespeare's Mark Antony notwithstanding, the good you and I do does live after us.* Because personality and character survive as precious to God's purposes, so also our individuality survives. We shall all know one another in eternity with the same sureness we have known one another on earth.

This means that neither you nor I need be afraid of death, in whatever form it may threaten or finally come. For God will bring the fine, enduring fruits of our life safely into His barn. The essential values we have grown into our souls will be spared the disintegration of the grave. What is eternal in us will pass into the nearer presence of the Lord. Your task and mine, then, is to build more stately mansions for our souls through the days which remain to us.

When David Livingstone reached the heart of Africa, he asked the inland natives, "What becomes of the Congo River?"

Never having heard of the Atlantic Ocean, they replied with expressive shrugs, "It is lost in the sands."

Just what becomes of your life and mine after the experience of death? We know "beyond a peradventure" that it is not lost in the sands, for Jesus has opened eternity to us. We rejoice that the Christlike parts of us pass over into new life, to serve the Lord in the company of other souls who, like our Savior, could not be held by death.

Thus you and I may cap our list of verities we most surely believe with the conviction of the survival of our personality after death.

> Then one of the elders . . . said to me, "These are they who have come out of the great tribulation; . . . They shall hunger no more, neither thirst any more;
> the sun shall not strike them, nor any scorching heat.
> For the Lamb in the midst of the throne will be their shepherd,
> and he will guide them to springs of living water;
> and God will wipe away every tear from their eyes" (Rev. 7:13, 16-17).

Notes

1. Poem by Kendrick Strong.
2. Words by John R. Rippon.
3. F. Van Wyck Mason, *Rascal's Heaven* (New York: Doubleday Company, 1964).
4. Fiorello LaGuardia, *The Making of an Insurgent: 1882—1919* (New York: J. B. Lippincott, 1948).
5. Arthur Hewitt, *Highland Shepherd* (New York: Willett & Clark, 1939).

BELMONT COLLEGE LIBRARY